THE DESERT AIR

NICHOLAS WRIGHT

A Methuen New Theatrescript
Methuen·London and New York

A METHUEN PAPERBACK

First published in Great Britain as a Methuen Paperback original in 1985 by
Methuen London Ltd, 11 New Fetter Lane, London EC4P 4EE and
in the United States of America by Methuen Inc, 29 West 35th Street, New York, NY 10001

Copyright © 1985 by Nicholas Wright

Wright, Nicholas, *1940-*
      The desert air.——(A Methuen new theatrescript)
      I. Title
      822'.914   PR6073.R52/

      ISBN 0-413-59880-2

Printed in Great Britain by Expression Printers Ltd, London N7

To Harry Wright

The Desert Air was first presented by the Royal Shakespeare Company at The Other Place, Stratford-upon-Avon, on 5 December 1984, with the following cast:

COLONEL GORE, *later* BRIGADIER GORE, *known as* HIPPO	Geoffrey Hutchings
MAJOR CARP, *his assistant*	Andy Readman
COMMANDER-IN-CHIEF, Middle East	Godfrey Kenton
HIS AIDE	Charles Millham
GENERAL BERNARD MONTGOMERY	David Whitaker
COLONEL JENIFER, *O/C Whiteworks*	Myles Hoyle
TIM PAGAN, *an officer in Dangerous Operations Groundforce*	Peter Eyre
MISS FIGGIS, *a senior secretary*	Polly James
CAPTAIN ADRIAN WOOLF, *responsible for Jugoslav/ Canadian volunteers*	Nicholas Woodeson
MAJOR PETER CRAGO, *an officer in the Jugoslav section of DOG*	Nicholas Farrell
CAPTAIN EDDIE FERGUSON, *Australian, a liaison officer to Jugoslavia*	Martin Jacobs
DR BABIC, *envoy in Cairo of the official Jugoslav resistance*	John Burgess
MR DJORDEJEVIC, *a Jugoslav partisan*	Peter Theedom
TWO MEN IN BOWLER HATS	Jonathan Scott-Taylor, Andy Readman
A TAXI DRIVER	Charles Millham
LUKA	Stephen Simms
BOGDAN	Jonathan Scott-Taylor
PETKO *Jugoslav/Canadian volunteers*	Andy Readman
JOSIP	Myles Hoyle
MILA, *a Polish refugee*	Cecile Paoli
JELKO, *another volunteer*	David Whitaker
MR LLOYD-LEIGHTON, *A Foreign Office official*	John Burgess
COLONEL VEATER, *an Intelligence officer*	Myles Hoyle
FRANCIS BOTHWELL, *a liaison officer to Jugoslavia*	Martin Jacobs

Staff officers, Yugoslavian/Canadian volunteers, taxi-drivers, restaurant customers, Intelligence officers, waiters: played by members of the company.

Directed by Adrian Noble
Decor by Chris Dyer
Lighting by Wayne Dowdeswell
Sound by John A Leonard
Music by Colin Sell

The play is set mostly in Cairo, in 1942/3.

The Desert Air subsequently opened at the Barbican Pit in summer 1985, in the same production.

ACT ONE

Scene One

Cairo 1942.

A parade ground. Officers enter and assemble in informal deferential order to MONTGOMERY, who is yet to arrive. The COMMANDER-IN-CHIEF (CIC) enters with his AIDE and takes the next most senior position. MONTGOMERY enters followed by AIDES.

MONTY: Good morning gentlemen.

Greetings follow according to rank. A map is set up on an easel, showing the intended battle area. MONTGOMERY demonstrates his tactic on it with his baton.

We shall launch our assault on Rommel's forces from the North. Rommel must suppose that we shall launch it from the South. The element of surprise is crucial. Our forces, poised for the Northern thrust, must be invisible to the enemy, (*To the* CIC:) eh?

CIC: Quite so.

MONTY: And what have your chaps come up with?

CIC (*to his* AIDE): Captain.

AIDE: The celebrated illusionist, Mr Jasper Maskelyne, has been working on the problem of the tank. We consider the tank, of all our armoured vehicles, the hardest to render invisible. Have you a moment now, sir, to inspect the prototype?

MONTY: Absolutely.

SOLDIERS *with white tapes cordon off* MONTY *and the other* OFFICERS. *Meanwhile:*

AIDE: Will you stand back please? (*To* MONTY:) If you wouldn't mind, sir. (*Calls to others:*) Very well back.

Everyone stands back.

(*To another* OFFICER:) Ready?

OFFICER (*calls*): Tank, please.

Pause. It's hot.

MONTY: Tch tch tch.

Two huge doors open and with an

immense din and clanking a tank rolls in, completely invisible, as described. Clouds of dust which make everyone cough. MONTY taps the tank with his baton, making a solid clang. All applaud, amazed, except for MONTY.

Very adequate. I must congratulate Mr Maskelyne. Where is he?

AIDE: Inside the tank, sir.

MONTY (*loudly*): Very well done, Mr Maskelyne.

MASKELYNE (*faintly from inside the tank*): Thank you very much, sir.

OFFICERS *applaud in delight.*

MONTY (*addresses everyone there*): The battle of El Alamein will be a rough-house. The German soldier is a bonny fighter and the only way to beat him is to kill him in battle. The secret is morale. We shall raise the character of our soldiery to the highest pitch. They look to us for strong and determined leadership and by Jiminy they shall get it.

ALL: Most refreshing/Bags-of-binge/Just what-the-doctor ordered/Mighty shake-up/keen as mustard/Greyhounds in the slips/ etc.

MONTY: Get rid of this.

The tank drives off, making clouds of dust and a tremendous noise as before. Everyone starts to leave, except: An intelligence officer lingers. He is COLONEL GORE, known as the HIPPO: a short, stubby, resentful regular soldier. With him is his assistant, MAJOR CARP. CARP is in his early thirties. He is in peace-time a college lecturer and has a Midlands accent.

CARP: Lunch, sir?

HIPPO: Wait.

He pats his swollen and distended stomach.

Look at that gut. Blown up like a fucking football. Know how big it is? A bile-duct? Size of a thumb. Gawd only knows what this one's up to.

He takes a pill.

Occurred to you to note, has it, Major Carp, that all great men are stumpies?

CARP: No sir?

HIPPO: Think of Napoleon, Churchill. Stalin. Hitler. And I've always pictured Jesus as a stumpy. I couldn't enter a church if I thought he was one of those long, tall, pointy bastards.

Monty is a stumpy. He is five foot four of concentrated zip and vigour. He has galvanised the Army. He has terrorised the Staff. And as for Rommel, he will knock him for six and out of Africa.

Tell me Major Carp: where will the *next* campaign take place?

CARP: In Europe?

HIPPO: Carp, you're learning. I intend to stake my claim on Europe before those pointy bastards get there. I have obtained a brand new posting. Here in Cairo. Dangerous Operations Groundforce.

CARP: DOG? Is that the best you could do, sir?

HIPPO: Strategy! DOG spells Europe. DOG sends *missions* to Europe. Greece, Hungary, Jugoslavia. It's a jampot. Have a cigar.

CARP accepts it: free cigars are unusual. CARP wonders what is pending. Lights it.

I like you, Carp. You're clever but it's not offensive. Scholarship boy. I spotted you when they posted you out as miserable captain. Raised you up, when not a bugger in the bar would bum a round off you, not with that accent. How's the cheroot?

CARP: Bit strong, sir.

HIPPO: You'll get used to it. I bring you tidings of an elevating nature. You will succeed me in my present post. You will be GSO (2) Intelligence Planning (Planning), rank of Lieutenant Colonel, goes with the job. You are looking at the man who swung it. Remember that.

CARP: I will, sir. Very chuffed indeed sir. Deeply grateful.

HIPPO: Twice a week, a package similar to this will be delivered to you by a major on a motorbike. Take a shufti.

He gives CARP an envelope. CARP reads the label.

CARP: SECRET.

The HIPPO's stomach gives him a twinge.

HIPPO: Open.

CARP opens it and finds another envelope inside and reads the label.

CARP: MOST SECRET.

The HIPPO'S stomach gives him a severe twinge.

You all right, sir?

HIPPO: The gut. Carry on.

CARP opens, finds another envelope inside and reads the label.

CARP: FOR COLONEL GORE'S EYES ONLY.

The HIPPO's stomach gives him a more severe twinge.

HIPPO: You have official clearance.

CARP opens and examines the contents. They are flimsy blue papers typed on in darker blue.

CARP: These are intelligence reports.

HIPPO: Note the format. Note the colour. They are enemy signals.

Beastly Hun, desiring to send a message, uses an enciphering machine. We, the great and good, possess a duplicate machine in Bletchley, Hertfordshire. We intercept the signal, feed it in, and all is revealed: positions of their troops. Their plots. Their plans. What Hitler had for breakfast. What you hold in your hand is the most terrifying secret of the war. Its name is Uncle Harry.

CARP: 'You must always believe what your Uncle Harry tells you'.

HIPPO: Eh?

CARP: It's a phrase from a book. *Three Men in a Boat.*

HIPPO: Bloody listen!

Uncle Harry is the truth. Now that you are on the circulation-list, you will never be removed. You will never see action. You will never be placed in any position where you might be captured by the enemy. You will live a life apart. Everyone else will seem to walk in darkness. You will long to tell the secret. It will gnaw your vitals. It will destroy your health.

There's only one cure. To tell it. As I have done to you, in the line of duty.

He flexes. Cheerful. The stomach pain has gone, the abdomen feels less distended.

Look at the gut. It's tickety-boo. And you, Carp?

CARP, *who is feeling ill, makes light of the fact.*

CARP: A little nauseous, sir. It's the cigar.

HIPPO: Don't count on it!

Scene Two

Out of the end of the previous scene: darkness and a hurricane bombardment. Flames, explosions, whizzing shells.
   The voice of a BBC radio announcement is heard:

'It has been announced that at 21.40 hours last night, the Allied Forces launched a major attack. Fighting is furious . . .'

A tranquil scene appears:
   LIEUTENENT COLONEL PAGAN'*s office at* DOG. PAGAN *and his friend* COLONEL TOBY JENIFER *are drinking cups of tea.*
   TIM PAGAN *is 43, cool, ascetic, subtly nervous. He is at this stage of his life neat and meticulous in his movements, dress and where he keeps things.*
   JENIFER, *a year or two older, is a worldly-looking figure. Both he and* PAGAN *were merchant-bankers in peace-time.*
   JENIFER *is in mid-flow:*

JENIFER: . . . so we put out a story that the English Channel was covered in some kind of oil and it would burst into flames upon command to repel invaders.

PAGAN: Did the Germans believe it?

JENIFER: Who can say, Tim, but the British public did. And the following week I got a telegram. Duty called, and could I fly out to Cairo to provide some equally cheerful scenarios about the new offensive.

   MISS FIGGIS *comes in. Early forties, wispy, secretively intelligent. She carries an armful of files.*

FIGGIS: May I disturb you? These are the briefing folders. Will you sign, please?

She gives them to PAGAN, *and opens the shutters to admit more light. Meanwhile:*

PAGAN: Thank you, Miss Figgis.

He signs in her little book of who's got what file. Meanwhile:

Tell me, Toby, are you free for lunch?

JENIFER: Oh not today. I'm meeting a colleague of ours from peace time. Reggie Matheson. Half past one. And then tonight I'm dining at Government House.

Pagan: What I'd like to chat about won't take long.

He gives MISS FIGGIS *her signing book back.*

That will be all.

He waits until she has gone; then addresses JENIFER *in confidential manner, choosing his words with care.*

We have a new appointment here at DOG. A regular officer. Colonel Gore. Known as the Hippo, not just aptly, really quite – profoundly on some atavistic level, and I honestly think he needs to be – contained in some way. Kept very busy perhaps or given nothing to do. I wondered, since you happen to be in Cairo, if I might pick your brains?

MISS FIGGIS *comes in.*

FIGGIS: It's me again. You asked me to say when Dr Babic arrived. I'll take your cups.

She comes into the room and starts to clear up. Meanwhile:

JENIFER: Shepheards, Long Bar, five past one precisely.

PAGAN: Splendid –

CAPTAIN ADRIAN WOOLF *comes in with a file: 30 or so, rumpled, wears spectacles, looks incongruous in uniform. He intends to talk to* PAGAN *about something quite different but –*

Woolf, the very fellow. Show Colonel Jenifer downstairs and sign him out please.

JENIFER (*to* PAGAN): Don't be late.

PAGAN: I never am.

WOOLF: This way, sir.

As WOOLF *and* JENIFER *go:*

PAGAN (*to* MISS FIGGIS*):* One moment, please.

They have gone. PAGAN *speaks in confidential manner once more.*

Does the Hippo plan to join us?

FIGGIS: Hard to say. He's frisky this morning. Burst in on the cipherines and made some rather unsuitable jokes. And then he kept the package.

PAGAN:Package?

FIGGIS: Didn't you hear? A major arrived on a motorbike with an envelope, and he wouldn't let me enter it in the daybook.

PAGAN:No no no, we can't have secret info floating about unfiled. Please talk to him.

The HIPPO *comes in.* PAGAN *rises.*

HIPPO: Good morning!

PAGAN: 'Morning.

HIPPO: Who's that old fart in the corridor?

PAGAN: Colonel Jenifer. He and I were fellow bankers. And the best of friends. Won't you sit down.

HIPPO: Thank you.

He sits in PAGAN's *chair, and takes a sheaf of Uncle Harry papers out of his briefcase. Studies them.*

FIGGIS: Your briefing folder.

She offers the HIPPO *a briefing folder. He opens it in annoyance.*

HIPPO: : What are these?

FIGGIS: Documents on the current state of play in Jugoslavia.

HIPPO (*to* PAGAN, *suspicious*): Think I'm stupid?

PAGAN: Certainly not. I find them useful.

HIPPO: Thank you. I have my own.

He puts the folder aside, and examines his Uncle Harry papers, spreading them over the desk, making sure they can't be overlooked. Gets more out of his briefcase and adds them to the display. PAGAN *and* MISS FIGGIS *watch, impressed but concerned. The* HIPPO *becomes aware of them.*

(*To* FIGGIS): What are you gawping at?

FIGGIS: Should I not put those papers through the system?

HIPPO: They're secret.

FIGGIS: We are a secret unit.

HIPPO: OUT!

As she goes:

Nosey old cow.

PAGAN: Miss Figgis is our resident filing wizard. She has a private system. Very effective –

HIPPO: DOG is not a village library. It's a machine of war. It will be tuned up in the Monty fashion –

ADRIAN WOOLF *comes in. He's alarmed at finding that he's interrupted the* HIPPO.

What d'you want?

WOOLF: I'm sorry. (*To* PAGAN:) You asked for a memo, sir, on discontent amongst our volunteers. It's here. No, here. Collected fruits of a democratic meeting –

HIPPO: Damn you, hoppit!

WOOLF *goes quickly.*

Bolshevik. Hebrew Bolshevik. Spot 'im a mile off. Have him seen to.

PAGAN: Captain Woolf is highly capable. I happen to know his father and he –

HIPPO: Shut your cake'ole!

PAGAN *stops. The* HIPPO *smiles.*

Before I change my mind. I bring you tidings of an elevating nature.

PAGAN: What?

HIPPO: You have been promoted to the rank of colonel.

PAGAN *is taken aback.*

PAGAN: Have my duties altered?

HIPPO: No.

PAGAN: Why the change?

The HIPPO *searches* PAGAN's *face for signs of idiocy or cunning. He finds neither.*

HIPPO: I have been mugging up on

Europe. DOG has officers in the field. Dummett in Greece and Pincher in Albania. It is essential for their standing amongst the locals that they rise to colonel. You're their senior officer and must rise accordingly.

PAGAN: Merely technical? Then I shan't object.

HIPPO (*furious*): Object!

CAPTAIN FERGUSON *comes in: Australian, young, self-reliant. He is in full battledress. With him is MAJOR PETER CRAGO, late twenties.*

PAGAN: Come in, come in. (*To the* HIPPO;) Colonel, you've not met Captain Ferguson, who is to be parachuted into Jugoslavia tonight.

FERGUSON (*to the* HIPPO): Nice to meet you at last, sir.

PAGAN *speaks into his desk telephone:*

PAGAN: Will you send in Dr Babic please? (*To* CRAGO:) Is everything in order, Major Crago?

CRAGO: We're driving Eddie to the airfield in time for a drink in the Wing-Commander's office. Take-off's at eight. He'll be dropped at approximately three am, as long as the weather holds and the pilot can see the signal fires.

PAGAN: No other problems?

CRAGO: I only wish I was going.

PAGAN (*with sympathy*): Next time, perhaps. Eddie, you're kitted up?

FERGUSON: Been packed for days, sir. I've been writing letters all morning. Bit of a dodge, to stop my dear old mum from wondering where I've got to. And every month, Peter's gonna post one back to Melbourne, so she gets a colourful account of what a find old time I'm having in Cairo.

PAGAN: Quite a feat of the imagination.

HIPPO: Yes, there's a limit to what one can say about food and fucking. Where's that Jug?

MISS FIGGIS *shows* DR BABIC *in and leaves.* DR BABIC *is middle-aged, thoughtful, well-groomed but shabby.*

PAGAN: Dr Babic, thousand welcomes.

May I present our new Military Director, Colonel Gore. Captain Ferguson. Major Crago, our GSO 2 Jugoslavian desk. I've been meaning to say –

DR BABIC *settles down.*

– that in real life, I frequently wrote to a *Mr* Babic of the Imperial Bank, Belgrade. Are you related?

BABIC: My brother.

PAGAN: Is he well?

BABIC: He was killed in the bombing.

HIPPO (*impatient at this waste of time*): Can we get on, please?

PAGAN: You have a statement, Doctor?

As BABIC *continues, the* HIPPO *sorts his papers out.*

BABIC: Thank you.
In April 1941, when Jugoslavia was invaded by the Germans, a resistance army was formed under the leadership of a mighty patriot, General Draza Mihailovic. He and his followers – *Chetniks,* as they are called – have waged a bitter struggle from their stronghold on Mount Durmitor. I speak on his behalf, to thank you, Captain Ferguson for joining him in arms.

PAGAN: I am honoured to affirm His Majesty's Government's support for the Chetnik army in its gallant struggle.

PAGAN *looks at his watch: plenty of time to get away and meet* TOBY JENIFER. *But: the* HIPPO *sings to himself in pantomimed long-suffering:*

HIPPO: 'Oh God our help in ages past . . .'

PAGAN: Do you wish to add anything?

HIPPO: No no.

PAGAN (*to* BABIC): Then, Dr Babic, I thank you for attending and –

HIPPO: (*suddenly impatient*): You're pulling our legs of course, about the gallant struggle? Because at GHQ the word on the Chetnik army is they haven't fired a shot.

FERGUSON: Isn't this what I'm meant to be finding out.

HIPPO: Shut up !

FERGUSON: I –

HIPPO: Nothing to do with you!

BABIC: Excuse me. This young man, he must find out what?

An awkward moment. PAGAN addresses him as one reasonable man to another.

PAGAN: I cannot deceive you. Captain Ferguson is to ascertain whether the arms, explosives, heaven knows what else, which we've been sending the Chetniks for the last twelve months have been put to use. If he reports that the resistance is in fact resisting, we shall send a full-scale military mission in support. If he finds no evidence of combat, we shall not.

BABIC shifts ground: cautious, persuasive.

BABIC: Draza Mihailovic is not a Balkan warrior from the comic books. He is an intellectual. He takes no pleasure in the sight of blood. I speak of the blood of peasants. Already the Germans have slaughtered half a millon. Women, children. These are killings in reprisal. They are punishments for reckless attacks on enemy targets. What is the point of such attacks when the only result is the killing of innocent people? People who will betray us if we risk their lives. Once we are prepared, once we are strong, then we shall fight.

HIPPO: Oh pig shit. What I suggest, we cut our losses, send this wombat – (*He indicates FERGUSON.*) to some sensible bloody country –

PAGAN: Dear oh dear.

HIPPO: What about Greece?

FERGUSON: I don't speak Greek.

PAGAN: He only speaks Australian and Serbo-Croat.

HIPPO (*brightening suddenly*): Hold it! I see the light. 'Reckless attacks on enemy targets.' Just the job, precisely what we're looking for. Who did them? Crago!

CRAGO: We don't exactly know what's happening there.

FERGUSON: Not *yet* -

HIPPO: *Be quiet.*

Pause. PAGAN looks nervously at his watch.

CRAGO: There's a radio station, which the Nazis jam. But it seems to report a separate force, quite different from the Chetniks. Opposed to them in fact. It calls them partisans. And claims they're fighting the Germans. Now.

HIPPO: Chetniks, Partisans. Good Jugs, bad Jugs, which is which?

PAGAN: Might I suggest: this very complex picture can't be approached on a cowboys and Indians basis. Colonel Gore, you have a briefing folder, given you by the excellent Miss Figgis. Please consult it.

The HIPPO cross-refers to his Uncle Harry papers. Looks from one to the other and quickly loses track of what's in which pile.

As for you, Major Crago. Radio Free Jugoslavia is a Soviet propaganda stunt. According to them, the heroic masses have risen by the thousand. Hitler trembles. Ammo-dumps are going up in flames like bonfire night. We don't believe it. Partisans there may be, in scattered groupings, but their military weight is nil.

HIPPO (*armed with an as yet unseen piece of paper, pounces*): Then what are twenty German divisions doing in Jugoslavia? Winter sports?

This figure surprises everybody: their estimate is much lower.

PAGAN: Who says twenty?

HIPPO: I do. You do. In your briefing folder!

He hands PAGAN a blue Uncle Harry paper, as:

PAGAN (*to CRAGO*): What's our estimate?

CRAGO: Five.

HIPPO (*sees PAGAN holding the blue paper and snatches it back*): So it is. Positive I'd seen the figure twenty. But I can't say where.

He clutches his stomach in pain.

Oh blast.

He quickly hides the Uncle Harry document and takes a pill.

BABIC: The partisans are bandits. My General is to them a symbol of our King, our Church, our cultural traditions. They attack us! Never will there be peace until they are destroyed.

PAGAN: On the contrary.

HIPPO (*in pain*): Ooh!

PAGAN: Bandits or no, your general will invite them to regroup beneath the Chetnik banner. Captain Ferguson will so instruct him –

FERGUSON: Thanks a bunch!

PAGAN: Mihailovic is our ally. He and only he will lead a united resistance whether or not he wants to. This is British Foreign Policy. It cannot change.

HIPPO (*thoughtfully*): Quite so.

BABIC (*with spirit*): Enough! I radio tonight. They will light no signal fires, he cannot land. Who do you think we are to order us so? Are we your allies? Or are we merely foreigners?

The HIPPO *intervenes with supreme aplomb.*

HIPPO: You are foreigners. *You* are a very funny foreigner. Who pays your salary? The British Government. If you don't like us you can fuck yourself.(*He takes a pill. To everyone*:) I have familiarised myself with the Jugland picture. Ferguson will join the Chetniks. (*He turns to* BABIC.) A military mission of gigantic strength will follow. Men, supplies and *cash*.

BABIC: Is this a promise?

HIPPO: Gentleman's honour.

BABIC *is about to embrace him in thanks but:*

Hands off! Ferguson, bugger off fast. Crago, your shirts's hanging out.

PAGAN (*to* FERGUSON): Eddie, good luck. (*To* BABIC): Doctor we shall –

HIPPO: Yes, yes, yes.

FERGUSON, CRAGO *and* DR BABIC *leave.* PAGAN *stays. The* HIPPO *glowers at him.*

That woman.

PAGAN: Do you mean Miss Figgis?

HIPPO: Mucking about with classified material. Give her the chop.

PAGAN: Where would she go?

HIPPO: Who cares? And keep that greasy Jugoslav out of my sight in future.

PAGAN: I certainly shall. He isn't used to being spoken to in that fashion.

HIPPO: Carrot and stick.

PAGAN: When does he get the carrot? The military mission you announced? I hardly think you'll send it if it can't be justified.

HIPPO: It will be justified! By me! To the Commander-in-Chief if necessary! I'm after the big stuff! (*With derision.*) Look at Ferguson. Miserable bloody *Captain*. What's that add to the greater glory of DOG? Sweet Fanny Adams. (*He comes to the point:*) Each of our missions to each of our Balkan clients must be commanded by an officer of senior rank.

PAGAN: You're hardly suggesting that we build up the mission so the officer in command can be promoted?

HIPPO (*exasperated*): Jumping Jiminy Cricket, that's the point! And where's my thanks? I slog and sweat to earn a modicum of respect for this pipsqueak unit. Look at you! A Colonel! Who swung that? Who did the wangle?

PAGAN (*angry*): I didn't sign up in order –

HIPPO: You despise me.

PAGAN *backtracks with lightning speed.*

PAGAN: No I –

HIPPO: *Don't tell me you never bloody wangled, you're a banker.*

PAGAN *chooses his words with care, torn between handling the* HIPPO *and being strictly truthful.*

PAGAN: There's a lot of nonsense talked about merchant banking. One never wangles. Never deceives. One's dealing all the time with friends. With men of one's social circle. If you can't trust friends, you might as well shoot yourself. If they can't trust you, you do shoot yourself. It's different I know for the professional soldier. One must compromise. (*Makes a daring leap.*) Miss Figgis. Can I not let her stay pro tem? I'm sure you'll find her less annoying if she's kept on a shorter rein. Her filing system's half the trouble, nobody understands it. I could scrap it at once. I shall.

HIPPO: Have it your own way.

PAGAN: Thank you (*He looks at his watch.*) One o'clock. I must lock the office.

HIPPO: Care for lunch?

PAGAN: I'm meeting a friend at Shepheards, I'm afraid. I'm sorry.

The HIPPO is wounded by this snub, but:

HIPPO: You'll have a snort, though.

He produces as though by magic a flask of whisky.

PAGAN: If you –

HIPPO: Bloody close eh?

He closes the shutters. PAGAN produces two hairbrushes from their usual place and starts to brush his hair prior to going out. The HIPPO watches him with interest. Meanwhile:

Where to eat? Perennial problem. The Anglo-Egyptian club is full of brainy buggers. Where's your crockery?

PAGAN: Left-hand drawer.

The HIPPO finds the glasses and pours drinks. Meanwhile:

HIPPO: Groppi's is full of queers and Jew-boys. Hate them. I hate lots of people. Women who deny their femininity. Wogs who deny their wogness. People who get their faces in the paper. Heroes. Tall men. Pointies. (*With some savagery.*) You are happy to be a colonel provided it is I who do the dirty work.

PAGAN: I do not follow you.

HIPPO: Drink.

PAGAN: Oh, thank you.

PAGAN, *who is in fact a drinking man, finishes the whisky in one gulp. The HIPPO notices this with interest.*

HIPPO: What one lacks is a pal to jaw with. Don't you find? I tell you what. I'll toddle along to Shepheards with you. Meet your chum and treat you all to a bite.

PAGAN (*mutters to himself*): Oh God how frightful!

HIPPO: Eh?

PAGAN *privately horror-struck at the thought of introducing the HIPPO to JENIFER, let alone REGGIE*

MATHESON, *thinks fast and replies pleasantly:*

PAGAN: He's rather a bore. We could eat elsewhere, you and I.

HIPPO: I'm comfy here. And you?

PAGAN: Oh yes.

He sits. The HIPPO pours more whisky for each of them. They drink. The HIPPO begins a fantastically involved and boring story.

HIPPO: I remember once, when I was in Addis Ababa –

Scene Three

A cell in Wandsworth Prison. A Jugoslav in his thirties, MR DJORDEJEVIC, *is being interviewed by two men in bowler hats. They are reasonably pleasant ex-Indian Army policemen.* DJORDEJEVIC *is helpful but very tough.*

BOWLER-HAT 1: You will not discuss your war activities with the other prisioners. That is why you are here in Wandsworth Prison, to keep them secret.

BOWLER-HAT 2: Ready, Mike?

BOWLER-HAT 1 *prepares to take notes.*

DJORDEJEVIC: My birthplace is Crnacko Polje, in Croatia. But I was, till April 1940, projectionist at the cinema in Svilajnec.

BOWLER-HAT 2 (*anticipates difficulty with spelling*): I'll do it, Mike.

He takes the notebook.

DJORDEJEVIC: This is how I learn to speak English, from the subtitles. When the Germans attack Jugoslavia, the cinema close. No electric current. Every day now, people in my town are disappearing. I ask, 'Where is Mr So-and-so?' They answer, 'He has gone to join the partisans'. May 28th I join the partisans. Our HQ is in the forest. We clear the woods, build walls. June 22nd, we advance on Macva district. Here we free the villages and open the banks, to pay the labourers who make our weapons.

The Germans come back. We hide. In Kragujevac they shoot all the students of gymnasium age from Grade 1 to Grade 8 -

BOWLER-HAT 1: How many partisans were there?

DJORDEJEVIC: In my detachment, three hundred and twenty men. If you ask in the country – ? Oh. One million.

BOWLER-HAT 2 (*looks at his watch*): Nine am tomorrow.

He knocks on the door. A prison warder opens it. DJORDEJEVIC *goes out.*

BOWLER-HAT 1 (*to* BOWLER-HAT 2): Same old cock and bull.

Scene Four

PETER CRAGO *meets* ADRIAN WOOLF.

WOOLF: Major Crago?

CRAGO: Captain Woolf.

WOOLF: Our taxi, sir.

There is a taxi waiting. They climb in.

Ready, driver

TAXI-DRIVER: Yes please.

WOOLF: Straight down the Giza Road as far as the Pyramids.

TAXI-DRIVER: Five piastres.

WOOLF: Right you are, let's go.

The taxi starts and they drive off with much jerking and bouncing on potholes and avoiding deadly traffic.

TAXI-DRIVER: I show you Pyramids ten piastres.

CRAGO: Do explain.

WOOLF: We do not wish to see the Pyramids. Lovely though they are. Our destination is a stucco-fronted house quite near, called Sunrise Villas.

TAXI-DRIVER: Sunrise Villas is no longer girlie house.

WOOLF: We know that thank you.

TAXI-DRIVER: Sunrise Villas is now top secret house for men who train to fight the Germans in Jugoslavia.

WOOLF: Well take us there all the same would you be so kind?

They settle down as the taxi drives on, swerving and bumping.

CRAGO: You can drop the sir.

WOOLF: Oh, good.

CRAGO: You can call me Crago.

WOOLF: Can I indeed, then let me tell you, Crago, that your behaviour was appalling.

CRAGO: When?

WOOLF: Oh don't pretend. Remember the day you started at DOG?

CRAGO: Of course.

WOOLF: I was in the map room reading *Tribune* and you took one look and leapt into Pagan's office and said, 'I ought to warn you, sir, that I have just observed a well-known Communist, Adrian Woolf'!

CRAGO: That's exactly what you were at Trinity.

WOOLF: So I told him. And he said he knew there was lots of that at Cambridge and it wouldn't be fair if my career was blighted by an adolescent phase. I mean how insulting, and I might have lost my job!

CRAGO: I was doing my duty.

WOOLF: Rot.

A blare of horns as an approaching car nearly crashes into them. They duck in terror, then continue.

I can't help wondering what your interest is in me, or Sunrise Villas.

CRAGO: Last resort. I've had a rotten war so far. Stuck behind a stupid desk. If I don't get a spot of action soon I'll miss the whole damn show. So what I planned was to go on a military mission to Jugoslavia.

WOOLF: Will there be one?

CRAGO: Not on present form.

WOOLF: Why? What does Ferguson say?

CRAGO: He found the Chetniks. And they won't let him off Mount Durmitor. He's seen no evidence of fighting, and they tell him nothing and it's all a washout.

WOOLF: How can I help?

CRAGO: I thought there was just a chance that one of your volunteers might know what's happening there. And if they do, I'll use it to persuade the Brigadier.

WOOLF: What Brigadier?

CRAGO: The Hippo. Didn't you know? He's been promoted.

WOOLF: Isn't that rather strange?

TAXI-DRIVER: Look out! The Pyramids!

WOOLF: STOP!

The next locale assembles: a group of Canadian Jugoslavs, very tough, fit and rugged, in deference to WOOLF *whom they like and admire. Meanwhile:*

Sunrise Villas was, as the driver said, a knocking-shop, pre-war, and it still has frilly lampshades up and peepholes in the doors. Last year they booted out the girls and put my charges in. Their total strength is twenty-two. Some have gone for parachute-training, some are learning how to capture a village, three have dysentry – (*He introduces a group of them.*) These are Petko, Luka, Bogdan, Josip.

CRAGO *shakes hands with them.*

Shall we be seated?

They settle down. CRAGO *proceeds.*

CRAGO: I know that none of you volunteers have seen Jugoslavia since you were, er, Kids. But you all have family ties there. This is why we recruited you in Canada – I'm sorry, have I said something funny?

After a pause, LUKA, *who is leader-for-the-week, replies:*

LUKA: We signed up in Canada back last year. For why? So's the British could train us up to fight the Nazis. We turn in our jobs and kiss bye-bye to our wives and kiddies. And we come out here to Cairo. We wanted to fight, that right, fellers?

OTHERS: Right/Dead right, pal.

BOGDAN: Only no dice. We've been sitting on our butts nine months. Why in hell ain't we in Jugoslavia?

PETKO: Are the British afraid or what?

ANOTHER: Is Mr Churchill playing us all for suckers?

ANOTHER: We're cheesed off.

Uproar.

CRAGO: Good, fine, now will you listen?

I'm the officer responsible for Jugoslavia. I'm as keen as any of you to send a military mission. And it'd help a lot if any of you chaps have recent news about what's going on. Messages from your parents, perhaps, or friends?

PETKO: This mission, where you plan to send it?

CRAGO: Oh, to the Chetniks.

ALL: Never/no dice/Baloney/Bullshit/ Crap/forget it, baby!

LUKA: Comrades!

They fall silent. He addresses CRAGO:

Our parents loved our country. Why then did they sail for Canada? Because life at home had become intolerable. They were being chased for too much dough by a landlord. The King was taking their kiddies to fight in the army. They wanted freedom. Now you ask yourself, did we volunteer to fight for what, the Chetniks, or for guys like us?

PETKO: Exploiters or the masses?

ALL: Sure/Right on/Better believe it/You think about it, comrade.

CRAGO: No this won't do, 'cos all of us are fighting Hitler, and the broader issue –

WOOLF: Hang on, Peter. Where is Jelko?

BOGDAN: Jelko got upset.

PETKO: He's got an uncle –

LUKA: - used to work the projector at the moviehouse in Svilajnec. And he got to Britain somehow and he wrote to Jelko –

CRAGO: Wrote a letter?

LUKA: Sure.

CRAGO: Where is it?

WOOLF: Where is Jelko?

BOGDAN: Gone into town.

WOOLF: A taxi!

The scene dissolves as WOOLF *addresses the volunteers.*

Town is out of bounds for all you comrades. There's a Chetnik spy, one Dr Babic, rabid fascist, if he knows we're training you up he'll blow his top –

LUKA: We come to help you look!

WOOLF: All right, get in.

In the taxi. CRAGO, WOOLF, LUKA, BOGDAN. LUKA *is explaining to* CRAGO:

LUKA: The anti-Nazi struggle cannot be won by a system in decay –

CRAGO: What system's that?

WOOLF: Just listen.

LUKA: - the ruling classes need the energies of the workers and the peasant strata -

BOGDAN: Don't forget the colonial oppressed, comrade.

LUKA: Sure –

WOOLF: Jelko's probably gone to Groppi's –

LUKA: The war has progressed beyond its limited objective, see –

CRAGO (*to* WOOLF): Is this what you're teaching them?

LUKA: - it is a war against oppression of every kind. It is a war for people's liberation.

WOOLF: -or perhaps the Kit-Kat.

BOGDAN: - people's control of the products of their labour.

WOOLF: You see the contradiction, Peter? Once Europe is free, what happens to the right-wing governments? What happens to your precious kings?

BOGDAN: Out of a job!

WOOLF: To take an example, when the Polish people offer a fraternal embrace to the Soviet Union -

LUKA: Here we are!

The taxi stops with a jerk.
Groppi's. Music. Evening. Lots of customers: officers on leave, rich Levantines. Tables, umbrellas. CRAGO *and* WOOLF *at a table with milk shakes.* LUKA *and* BOGDAN *disappear into the crowd.*

WOOLF (*to* LUKA *and* BOGDAN): Circulate discreetly and report back here, this table will be base.

They sidle off, examining the other customers.

Soggy cake, decayed umbrellas. Odd, don't you think, that Groppi's is so famous? The chaps in the desert imagine swaying palms and dancing fountains.

CRAGO: I expect they imagine women.

WOOLF: There, I'm told, it proves its reputation to the hilt.

MILA, *a very attractive Polish girl of 20, approaches them.*

MILA: May I sit here? I wish to appear accompanied.

A waiter is at the table.

CRAGO: What would you like?

MILA: A raspberry ice. I'm starving.

CRAGO (*showing off his Arabic*): Ezma! Wahad ice-cream pink-one.

WAITER (*who used to wait at the Connaught Hotel*): One raspberry ice? Of course, sir.

The waiter goes.

MILA: I have escaped from Poland. Warsaw. Very beautiful. It is full of Jews but lovely in the summer. See, I have a brooch. (*She shows them.*) It was given me by my grandmother on her deathbed. Will you buy it? I am desperate. I have been robbed. Some damned Egyptian peasant.

WOOLF: How did you escape?

MILA: Through Czechoslovakia, Hungary, Roumania, Bulgaria.

WOOLF: All those countries are packed with Nazis.

MILA: So I noticed.

CRAGO: Weren't you afraid?

MILA (*with aplomb*): Of course!

LUKA *and* BOGDAN, *who have got themselves drinks, come back.*

LUKA: There is no evidence of comrade Jelko.

BOGDAN: I suggest the Continental.

WOOLF: Far too grand.

MILA: Let's go! (*To* LUKA *and* BOGDAN:) Call a taxi.

In the taxi. LUKA, BOGDAN, CRAGO, WOOLF *and* MILA. MILA *is eating her ice-cream and waving the spoon for emphasis. The taxi bumps and swerves from side to side.*

MILA: I fled to find the British Army. And my husband. He is English -

CRAGO: Is he in Cairo?

MILA: I don't know. We met in Warsaw, in a popular cafe. I was eating a raspberry ice. We called for another spoon and we fell in love. Domestic life was paradise. One weekend he was summoned back to London. Two days later, bang, the Germans begin bombardment. Come the tanks. No letters, telephone pfoo. One morning I opened my bathroom window. Out in the street there is an SS officer, he say to another one, today we raid all houses in this street. My papers are prepared. I go. I travel, one year. Tomorrow I will shout at the fools in the British Embassy. My husband is distinguished. He is obsessed by what is physical. He was contemptuous of the Polish men, he said they had no grasp of the romantic spirit. He dance on a table, he take me to a public place and touch my titties. You may have this brooch for a thousand piastres. Or I take sterling.

CRAGO: I can't afford it.

WOOLF (*firm*): Neither can I.

CRAGO: If you've nowhere to stay, I can offer you a shakedown.

MILA: You will jump on me, it will be too boring. (*To* WOOLF:) I stay with you.

CRAGO: Why him?

MILA (*as to an idiot*): Because he is an obvious *pederaste*!

LUKA/BOGDAN (*to* TAXI-DRIVER): Stop! Hold it! Here we are!

The taxi stops.

WOOLF: Not a minute too soon. Comrades, fan out.

In the Continental. Lots of customers. More British officers. CRAGO *and* WOOLF *at a table. A waiter is there. The remains of* MILA*'s ice on the table.*

WAITER: Brandy mafinish.

CRAGO: Any scotch?

WAITER: Maltese whisky.

WOOLF: Two.

WAITER *goes.*

CRAGO (*looks for* MILA): She's trying to flog the brooch. Do you think it's real?

WOOLF: You can buy them for ten piastres down the road. Ask me another.

CRAGO: How can I send a mission when the Jugs won't fight the Germans?

WOOLF: My Jugs will. It's only World War II that's stopping them.

CRAGO: Mihailovic won't fight.

WOOLF: You bet. You can't fight guerrilla war if you don't have popular support. Resistance in Jugoslavia is being waged by a people's army.

CRAGO: How do you know?

WOOLF: I have deduced it into being.

CRAGO: What do you know about the partisans?

WOOLF: Nothing at all. Do tell.

CRAGO: There's a Soviet radio stunt keeps on about them.

WOOLF: And?

CRAGO: The day Eddie Ferguson was dropped, the Hippo let slip that there are twenty German divisions in Jugoslavia.

WOOLF (*whistles*): How does he know?

CRAGO: He has a secret source.

WOOLF: And *who* - is tying these twenty divisions down?

CRAGO: The partisans. It must be.

WOOLF *is moved, excited.*

WOOLF: God, how thrilling. Theory becoming fact before one's eyes. A people's army. *Proved.* All that I've intuited from my team. My Jugs. My comrades. Real at last. Their hopes aren't wasted. All their energy, their zeal, is shared. A peasant-proletarian rising!

He stands on the table, completely carried away. CRAGO, *by way of making light of this, applauds. The other customers join in.* WOOLF *climbs down, and continues:*

As I predicted. How I love them. Can you imagine how my knees collapsed the day I met them. My first lecture. What I had decided, I would go for broke. Engels.

'Peasant Revolt'. And they adored it. Missed their lunchbreak. Imagine undergraduates, if I chose that subject, how they'd rag me. And I'd done some talks in Bermondsey, anti-Mosley stuff, and they were no great shakes, I couldn't get the accent right. Oh thank you.

Their drinks have arrived. They drink.

What I have done: is fall in love with the human race. And if what one is, is a Jewish Hampstead swot who cannot kick a ball straight, then it's glorious when your affections are returned.

CRAGO (*who has been worrying about this*): Are you really a queer?

WOOLF: Do you want to know?

CRAGO: No. It's irrelevant.

WOOLF (*taps his head*): It's here. (*Taps his heart.*) And here. (*Laughs.*) Oh yuk!

CRAGO (*with sympathy*): I'm awfully sorry.

WOOLF: I'm fantastically happy, you fool!

TIM PAGAN *is seen. He is a bit tight, and also looks drawn and tired.*

CRAGO: Look out! Tim Pagan.

PAGAN *approaches.*

PAGAN: Peter. Adrian. Drink?

He sits at their table.

CRAGO: There's only bogus whisky.

PAGAN: No, no, no, there's creme de menthe. (*To the* WAITER:) Same all round. (*To* CRAGO *and* WOOLF:) Have you had a nice evening?

CRAGO: Yes sir.

WOOLF: Fascinating.

PAGAN: Would you believe, it's midnight and I've only just left the Hippo's office. Poor man yearns for company. He closes the shutters. No escape. The image comes to mind of some Edwardian masher about to pounce on a chorus-girl. And then he talks. And talks. Awash with whisky –

The WAITER *is there with their drinks.* PAGAN *pays.*

I shouldn't be drinking this. (*He does:*) I do believe he's taken a sort of horrible shine to me. It's most oppressive. He has glistening hairs sticking out of his nostrils.

Fuzz on the backs of his thumbs. His eyes are pools of madness. God I'm hungry –

He sees the remains of MILA's *raspberry ice.*

Was that a raspberry ice?

He looks round for the WAITER *and sees* MILA.

PAGAN: How very odd. If it weren't for the dress, I'd swear that woman was my wife in Warsaw.

LUKA *and* BOGDAN *appear with* JELKO, *who is drunk.* MILA *sees* PAGAN.

MILA: Tim!

PAGAN: Mila?

WOOLF: Jelko!

CRAGO: Taxi!

Later. An empty street. Except for CRAGO, WOOLF *and* JELKO. JELKO *is sulking and silent: drink and black anger.* WOOLF *is looking after him.* CRAGO *is angry and depressed.*

WOOLF: Jelko's not at his best. He has a first-class brain.

CRAGO: Can he talk?

WOOLF (*belligerent*): He speaks excellent English. Don't you bastards understand a bloody thing? All bloody wogs the same, eh?

CRAGO: I'm only asking if he's sober enough to speak.

WOOLF: You ask him.

CRAGO (*to* JELKO): Where's that letter from your uncle?

JELKO: Wanna see it? Stick around, stick around.

Stands, staggers, takes out an envelope. Parodies an English upper-class accent.

Take a shufti, old sport.

CRAGO *opens the envelope and takes out the letter, which is on prison stationery, and has had nearly all the words cut by the censor, so it looks like a paper doily.*

JELKO: Fuck'n' censor.

WOOLF: Whatever he had to say was secret.

Pause. JELKO *sulks.* WOOLF *sits with him.*

CRAGO: There's a war going on. A millon miles away from stupid bloody things. My desk. The Hippo getting tidings of an elevatory kind. And all the time, somewhere out there, it's real. It matters. However horrible it is, however mad and frightening. Imagine what she's been through. How old do you think she is, nineteen? Incredible. I mean, what's Tim Pagan thinking of?

WOOLF: He was married before.

CRAGO: She liked me.

WOOLF: Well, she might be what you're after. I think *she's* quite mad and frightening –

CRAGO: Listen, will you? All this time in Cairo I've been wanting to fight. Patting myself on the back for being so *genuinely* keen. When Eddie went, I was sick with envy. Longing for him to sprain an ankle. Never once cared what side I'd be on. That's the stupidest bloody thing of all.

Pause. Then he speaks to WOOLF *with calm determination.*

How about this? Come down to the office. Soon as you like. We'll look through Eddie's signals. See what they say about the partisans. And tell the Hippo.

WOOLF: Fine! No, really, Peter. Marvellous.

CRAGO: That's on then. Good.

He looks around for something.

WOOLF: What?

CRAGO: A street sign.

WOOLF: You're down there.

He points down a street.

CRAGO: Good night

WOOLF: Good night, old bean.

CRAGO *goes.*

WOOLF: Jelko. Get up. I'm taking you back to Sunrise Villas.

JELKO: That's miles.

WOOLF: We'll get a taxi.

JELKO: Where's your apartment?

WOOLF: Quite near here as it happens. Why?

JELKO: Can I spend the night there?

WOOLF: Well, why not? And save the taxi-money. You could shakedown on the floor.

JELKO: I could. It ain't what I had in mind, though.

WOOLF: Can you clarify that?

JELKO: I'm saying I'd sure as hell be pleased if you and me was to go to bed together.

WOOLF: Jelko. Stop right there. Out of the question. Discipline out the window. That's the theory. Rubbish of course. The trouble is, I totally admire you. See the problem?

JELKO: Nope.

WOOLF: Me neither.

JELKO: Fine. Let's walk.

Scene Five

The HIPPO's *office at DOG. The* HIPPO *is about to give dictation to* MILA. *She is in a blouse and skirt. He is wearing his jacket, unbuttoned. As the scene progresses, he takes it off, revealing a dirty vest. It is night. He has a sheaf of papers: these are* FERGUSON's *signals, and he refers to them from time to time in a despairing way.*

HIPPO: Memorandum: to Intelligence Committee, GHQ. Subject: Funds and facilities for Military Mission to Jugoslavia.

MILA (*Writing*): GHQ.-

HIPPO: Ssh! (*Points to his forehead.*) Grey cells at work. Military mission costs a fortune. Molto Moolah, get the picture? GHQ must be convinced that what we send will be deployed. Convinced in writing, dammit. Hate memoranda. Always have done. Brain goes haywire at the sight of paper. Holy Moses, what comes next? Brain rebels at the sight of paper. Mm hm hm. (*He asks her*:) Reckon it's cold out there?

MILA: Naturally!

HIPPO: Here goes then 'Although our

liaison officer has been confined to Chetnik HQ by heavy snowfall –'

MILA (*writing*): liaisons officer–'

HIPPO: 'his opinion, Ferguson's, Captain's, Eddie's. Edward, Edwin, Figgis will know and something something spur to action.' Get me a cup of tea.

MILA: 'Get me a cup of –'

HIPPO: Don't write that!

MILA: Don't shout! Never not once in a thousand years has one of my family work for money! Tell me what you want to say, I do it.

HIPPO (*thinking this will floor her*): Ever written to a general?

MILA: Of course!

HIPPO: How did you start?

MILA: 'Mein lieber Pauli'.

HIPPO: That's German!

MILA: He was a German General!

HIPPO: Get me whatsisname. Your husband. Tell him I want him pronto, PDQ!

A knock on the door.

Yes!

It's PETER CRAGO *and* ADRIAN WOOLF. *They have a map of Jugoslavia, rolled up ready for display and a small collection of signals and other intelligence data.*

WOOLF (*moving past her*): Excuse me, Mrs Pagan –

CRAGO: Lovely evening –

HIPPO (*to* MILA): Out!

She leaves with style. Meanwhile:

Damn Polski nitwit. Shocking imposition on our hardpressed secretarial pool. Rule 23. 'Wives of officers may reside in Cairo *only* if engaged on vital work'. Tim Pagan knows this. He has *swung* her a job. He who never wangles. He has jeopardised internal admin for the sake of a poke. Almost makes you like the bastard. She's a goer! Notice the way she sucks her pencil?

CRAGO: Eddie Ferguson's signals –

HIPPO (*annoyed*): Yes?

CRAGO: Tuesday 22nd. Eddie reports a rumour at the Chetnik HQ, that the German airfield at Sarajevo has been attacked.

HIPPO: No doubt Ferguson got the dates wrong. (*He takes a pill.*)

WOOLF: Clearly the airfield was attacked by the partis –

HIPPO: Do not say it!

WOOLF: Partis – ?

HIPPO: They are a menace to law and order! Ferguson has betrayed me! Thousands of pounds it cost to send that Antipodean bumpkin. Weeks of effort. Down the khazi. Every signal more depressing than the last. I struggle and slave to find in – (*Seizes signals on his desk and waves them about.*) – all this hopeless, unencouraging bumf the slightest proof of combat. But I shall! I want a war out there! I want a *Bloodbath*!

FIGGIS *has just come in carrying a few files.*

FIGGIS: Your files. I'm sorry it took so long –

HIPPO (*who has grabbed them and seen the title of the top file*): I did not order the file on partisans!

FIGGIS: It's always called for sooner or later –

HIPPO: Scum! Filth! After the war we will shoot them in the streets like rats! (*Tears the file up in a rage and jumps on the remains.*) Ferguson's signals are not to circulate in unedited form! Fatal for morale! I'll receive them! You will not! When's the next transmission?

CRAGO: Half past ten –

FIGGIS: He's coming up now –

The HIPPO *dashes towards the door, seizing his pills, and saying –*

HIPPO: Don't let Pagan bunk off home. I need him.

He goes. FIGGIS *turns away.*

CRAGO: What a bastard.

WOOLF: Look.

They do. MISS FIGGIS *is in floods of silent tears, to their great embarrassment.*

CRAGO: Oh crikey.

WOOLF: Pat her on the back.

CRAGO: What, now? (*He doesn't.*) What a swine.

FIGGIS: Oh, I don't mind the *Hippo*.

She blows her nose. Recovers a bit.

I've had a shock, that's all. The files have been reorganised by Colonel Pagan. What can I say about the new arrangement? Very like him. Pedantic, boring, utterly without elan. Oh blast the man, he's trying to drive me out. (*She starts picking up bits of the torn-up file.*)They say I use a private system. It's a family system. My father's. A remarkable man. A professional amanuensis. He helped Mr Churchill, you know, on all his difficult books. You'd think it would suffice for a bogus colonel.

WOOLF: Miss Figgis?

FIGGIS: Yes?

WOOLF: Why is Pagan a bogus Colonel?

FIGGIS: Oh I can't say. It would be most disloyal. But since you insist, the Hippo was working Army Rules. Rule 187, subclause 2, and a grand old favourite of the Hippos of this world. (*She quotes without difficulty from memory*:) 'An officer who commands three other officers of identical rank –' – the same as his own, that is – shall automatically be promoted to whichever rank is next in seniority.' The Hippo wangled Colonel Dummett in Greece, Colonel Pincher in Albania and the third was Pagan.

WOOLF: And the Hippo went up to Brigadier.

FIGGIS: It always works in the hands of an expert.

WOOLF (*feels he's on to something*): The Hippo's an expert?

FIGGIS: Best I've seen since my days at the BBC.

WOOLF: What's his next move? If he wants to go up to Major-General –

FIGGIS: Three Brigadiers are needed.

WOOLF: Greece, no problem. Albania ditto. Jugoslavia!

CRAGO: That's why he wants the Chetnik mission –

FIGGIS: – which GHQ will never allow.

WOOLF: He'll send it to the partisans.

FIGGIS: He can't. He'll have to persuade the Foreign Office, Whitehall, GHQ.

WOOLF: He will! He *must*. He wants that third Brigadier. It's his overriding motivation. And history's on his side. We've reached that point, which comes in every British war, year three approximately, listen, Peter, when so many officers have been shot or sacked or led their regiments over cliffs, that there aren't enough left to fill the important jobs. It's also, of course, the point where we start to win. And why? Because the officers who take over are the Hippos. Sweaty little thugs from third-class regiments. Counter-jumpers. Opportunists. Men who've been snubbed and patronised for years. Men who can hate. It is the time of the Hippo! History is being moulded in their pachydermous paws. They are a *social movement. He's* a social movement. And if policy must be changed, he'll change it.

FIGGIS: I'm convinced.

CRAGO (*unsure at first*): I –. Yes. You're right. My mission! God I can't believe it. Jugoslavia! Yoohoo!

He calls out and leaps for joy. WOOLF dances about. PAGAN comes in looking shifty.

PAGAN: May I disturb the revels? I waited for the Hippo half an hour and left, is that quite clear?

The HIPPO comes in after him.

HIPPO: Ah, Tim–

PAGAN: Oh, God –

FIGGIS: Goodnight.

CRAGO:
WOOLF: } Goodnight, sir.

WOOLF, CRAGO and FIGGIS go. The HIPPO closes the shutters, making PAGAN miserable, and continues, finding the whisky meanwhile.

HIPPO: I've been trying to extract some sense from Ferguson's signals.

PAGAN: Are they not clear? The Chetniks haven't fought the Hun in living memory. Nobody wants a military mission more than I but–

HIPPO: Somebody does. Yours truly. I'm obsessed. I slaver. You'll have a snifter?

PAGAN: No, no whisky –

HIPPO (*who has already poured it*): Whoops! Too late, too late she cried – ! (*Gives* PAGAN *the glass.*) See the predicament, old boy, because I must request supplies. And I'd an excellent helper in my previous post, young Carp. No tone to the boy, no background worth a mousefart, but I miss him 'cos I'm all on my owneo, frightfully tizzed and I cannot compose the blinking memorandum to GHQ.

PAGAN (*who has been tipped off by* MILA): Are you ordering me to write it?

HIPPO: Asking. Jolly good practice.

PAGAN: No. I don't think so. No.

HIPPO *at first sympathetic.*

HIPPO: You're probably wise. 'Cause GHQ might say it's balls. Might sling it back at me, then you'd be tarred with the brush of failure. Bastards hate me. Total and utter swine. I slaved like a nigger in their miserable employ, and that's what they treated me like, a wog. Who worked late while they were propping up the bar at Shepheards? Who had to work from last year's calendar? Who got the ink with lumps in it? Muggins. Good old Hippo. Well it's been a very pleasant chinwag and you've drunk my drink and I think we have the basis for an understanding. I want total and unshaken loyalty personally to me. You write that memo.

PAGAN: No.

HIPPO: Why not?

PAGAN: It won't be true.

HIPPO: Calling me a liar?

PAGAN: Yes you are, you are the biggest liar in the Middle East.

HIPPO: And the best! Don't come it. How's your wife? How's her typing? I hear Miss Figgis had to help her find the question-mark!

PAGAN (*defensive*): Are you implying – ?

HIPPO (*friendly*): Fine by me! It's good to know you're human.

The HIPPO *pours* PAGAN *another whisky.*

PAGAN (*an admission*): You've never married?

HIPPO: Army.

PAGAN (*passes drink*): Thank you. (*Drinks it.*)

HIPPO: Never say no to a poke, mind. But it doesn't impinge. I use the time to solve some niggling problem. Know the feeling?

PAGAN *finishes his drink, moves it out of the* HIPPO*'s reach and moves to go.*

PAGAN: I'll tell my wife you're happy with her work. She'll –

HIPPO: Know how I joined the Army?

During the following he manages to fill PAGAN*'s glass somehow.* PAGAN *sits down slowly.*

My old dad was batman to an officer in the 2nd Wiltshires. Colonel Gore. I took the name in gratitude when he helped me into the regiment. Family name is Waters. I don't use it. Last time I saw my mum and dad, I hid behind a letterbox.

Gore had no descendants. When he died, he left my dad the contents of his house. Carpets, silver, furniture and paintings. Come the funeral, family Gore arrived. Oh what a flap. Had the old boy gone potty, leaving these priceless objects to an illiterate old man? They swiped the lot. They carried them down the stairs and into their waiting limousines. They gave my dad a cheque for fifty quid, which he thought was fair. And this is how I imagine that Sunday night. My dad in an empty house. Drinking his cup of tea. With not so much as a piece of brass to polish. Army gone. Master gone. As lost and - uncomprehending - as that dog, the late King George's doggie, at his funeral, when he trotted behind the coffin.

Never since then have I expected justice from my lords and masters. What have they done for me? I have been bilked and baulked and totally betrayed. By you! Your fellow pointy bastards! Nothing personal. I like you, Tim. Pig-ignorant, that's all. Live in a dreamworld. Things are ugly. I could wipe that look off your face like a fucking *rainbow*. Balkan revelations. I have a secret. (*A twinge of stomach pain.*) Jesus.

PAGAN: What?

HIPPO: The gut.

PAGAN: A secret?

HIPPO: Cannot tell you. No can do. The Chetniks – (*A severe stomach twinge. The pain continues in overwhelming waves as:*) Blimey. Terrible time last night. Hallucinated. Guess who I saw at the foot of my bed. Carp! E.F.Carp! Bobbing and beckoning like the ghost of Christmas past. Know what he said?

PAGAN: What?

Words erupt from the HIPPO's mouth as though he were possessed.

HIPPO: 'You must always believe what your Uncle Harry tells you!'

The pain has gone. He falls senseless to the floor.

PAGAN: Blast.

HIPPO (*sings*): 'Cobble and cobble as best I may
Cobble all night and cobble all day –' etc.

PAGAN (*mutters in exasperation*): Oh for God's sake.

The HIPPO awakes.

HIPPO: It's Tim! What did I say, Tim?

PAGAN: You sang the cobbler's song from Chu Chin Chow.

HIPPO: What else?

PAGAN: Who is Uncle Harry?

HIPPO: Ah.

He shakes himself. A sense of fresh air. Unlocks a drawer. Gets out lots of flimsy blue Uncle Harry intercepts. Gives them to PAGAN.

Read these. Then you can beetle off home.

PAGAN (*reads*): 'The 14th Panzer Division will reach Belgrade tomorrow'. When is tomorrow? (*He looks down the document.*) Today. These are enemy intercepts. (*Reads:*) They are calling up the Chetniks for assistance. (*Pause.*) Milhailovic is collaborating.

The Germans have twenty divisions there, you said. Is that the truth? (*Pause.*)The forces tying them down – the partisans are of equivalent strength? (*Pause.*)

It casts a very different light on your memorandum. (*Pause.*)

If we're to believe what our Uncle Harry tells us, there's a danger that the partisans might win.

I know Communists. You called me ignorant. So I was. Until a personal crisis. Very low ebb in my life, a messy divorce. I begged the bank to post me anywhere, ends of the earth. And settled for Budapest, then Prague, then Warsaw. And returned to life. Falling in love was half the trick. And conversation. And the richness of people's minds. And food and music, but I won't go on – And then one met, from time to time, the hardline Communist. One saw their dogmatism. Their intolerance of beauty. And their longing to destroy it if we let them.

HIPPO: And you'll write the memo?

PAGAN: I might help you with the phrasing. But my name must not appear.

He starts making notes on a memo pad. A very professional look to this. The HIPPO puts the whisky bottle within PAGAN's reach and leaves.

Scene Six

Wandsworth Prison. MR DJORDEJEVIC, the cinema-projectionist, continues his story, as though to the bowler-hatted men.

DJORDEJEVIC: Communists? Some partisans were so. They organise good, work hard. (*Indicates hard work with his arms.*) I am not a Communist. Nor anti-Communist. We fight together.

February 9th, I am captured by Chetniks. They beat me hard and send me to the prison camp in Beograd. We eat there once a day. One piece of bread, like so: (*He indicates the size.*) One litre of soup, no meat in it. There were many beatings. Many shootings. Many Jews were brought from a different camp on the site of the old fairground. All of them were shot.

April 21st, the Gestapo take us to be medically examined. Whoever could still walk was passed as fit. They say, you men will all do voluntary work. April 28th, we embark for Germany by ship. With me was one Radomir Boscovic: my best friend –

Scene Seven

A conference-room at GHQ. A large table around which are seated a number of high-ranking officers from different branches of Intelligence. They include CARP, a COLONEL VEATER, the HIPPO and PAGAN. A MR LLOYD-LEIGTON represents the Foreign Office. The meeting is being chaired by the COMMANDER-IN-CHIEF. His AIDE sits beside him.

CIC: DOG requests supplies for a mission to Jugoslavia. Everyone read the memo? (*Everyone has.*) Frankly, Brigadier Gore, I find it waffly. But the message is welcome. Captain Ferguson, you say, describes the Chetniks as a potent fighting force. Are there any comments?

CARP: Yes, sir.

AIDE (*murmurs to* CIC): Carp, Intelligence planning (Planning).

CARP: Brigadier Hippo –

HIPPO: Gore!

CARP: So sorry – Brigadier Gore suggests that that the number of German divisions in Jugoslavia is five or possibly six. Does he regard this estimate as complete?

The HIPPO's stomach gives him a spasm.

The figure accords with the Chetniks' modest military efforts up till now, but if –

HIPPO (*impatient, thumps the table*): Are you, are you querying the estimate?

CARP: Yes.

HIPPO: Then I must ask you, Lieutenant Colonel Carp, upon what basis?

CARP's stomach has a spasm. He speaks firmly.

CARP: I'd rather leave the basis out of it if I may.

CIC: Are you differently informed?

CARP *and* HIPPO *both take a pill.*

CARP: Brigadier Gore and I are identically informed this is what's so mysterious -

CIC: Are there German divisions in Jugoslavia which he does not mention?

CARP: I'm not at liberty to say, sir.

CIC: Then your objection's futile.

CARP: I'm afraid it is.

The HIPPO is delighted. Hums a merry tune and rubs his hands together.

LLOYD-LEIGHTON: Might I say –?

AIDE (*to* CIC): Mr Lloyd-Leighton, Foreign Office.

LLOYD-LEIGHTON: The Balkans are traditionally a murky area. Ancient feuds abound. Vendettas which cut across the official lines of battle. Might the result be – how shall I put it? – that the Chetniks response to the Hun invader is – ambiguous?

CIC (*to* AIDE): What's he on about?

AIDE: No idea, sir.

LLOYD-LEIGHTON: Is Mihailovic collaborating with the Germans? We wouldn't be shocked, if this were so, bearing in mind the historical context. But we wouldn't send him military aid, any more than we would to the Vichy French.

CIC: What grounds have you for this suggestion?

LLOYD-LEIGHTON: Well I can't say. One gets intelligence from so many sources these days.

He has an attack of wheezing. He gets out an asthma spray and sprays his throat. Meanwhile:

CIC: Brigadier Gore?

HIPPO: Colonel Pagan!

PAGAN *is caught in moral agony.*

CIC (*to* PAGAN): Well?

PAGAN: There is no evidence of collaboration.

An epidemic of symptoms passes around the table, leaving only the CIC and AIDE untouched. A COLONEL VEATER facial tic breaks out uncontrollably.

CIC: Any comments? (*He notices* VEATER.) Colonel Veater?

VEATER: Yes, sir?

CIC: You are winking at me.

VEATER: Not at all, sir. It's a nervous affliction. But since I have the floor, I'll turn if I may to the second page of Brigadier Gore's memorandum, where he quotes the attack on the German airfield at Sarajevo. A brilliant feat of arms. The question is, who did it?

HIPPO (*aggressive*): We say the Chetniks and so did the BBC.

VEATER: I -

HIPPO: Did you not hear the broadcast?

VEATER: I wrote the broadcast. I delivered the script, in London, in my taxi to the BBC, and had a long and frankly dreadful conversation with Sir John Reith, who said it was self-evident nonsense. I pointed out that the Chetniks were being credited, as so often, for political reasons, and he bowed to pressure. Never did I think the broadcast was correct. Yet here we find the myth perpetuated. Why?

AIDE (*to* CIC): The Yanks are waiting, sir.

CIC: Brigadier Gore: I can only authorise this mission with the full support of my Intelligence Staff. Clearly that support is lacking. Your request is therefore turned down. One final word. I suggest you note what Colonel Veater has implied, that some other crowd is doing the fighting. If this is so, a mission should be going to them.

The HIPPO *is suddenly riveted.*

HIPPO: Bloody marvellous! Brilliant, might I say so! Mission of course would need to be a large one. Senior status. Brigadier at the helm. Specifications, very much as outlined here – (*He indicates his memo.*) – fact of the matter, if I crossed out Chetniks where the word occurs and –

LLOYD-LEIGHTON: Are you suggesting a mission to Tito?

CIC: Who is Tito?

LLOYD-LEIGHTON: Happily I am authorised to answer this question.

Sources close to the enemy suggest a partisan force. Its size and effectiveness are irrelevant to this discussion, for the following reason:

Tito is not a woman, as we thought at first, nor indeed a man, but a committee. Tito is an acronym, like GHQ or DOG, and it stands for 'Tajna Internationalna Teroristicka Organizacija'. International Terrorism. A ruthless Politburo with the aim of spreading Bolshevisation

throughout the Balkan area. We at the Foreign Office must consider the kind of Europe we want to see after the war. Enslaved or free?

The question implies another. On whom can we depend to keep the flame of democracy alight? The answer is Mihailovic. No-one claims he's a very effective scourge of the Nazi horde. This is not his function. His function is to counter Communist influence, most especially when the war is over.

HIPPO: Can we not send a mission to the partisans?

LLOYD-LEIGHTON: Anthony Eden will not allow it.

CIC: If we want to beat the Russians, we shall have to beat the Germans first.

LLOYD-LEIGHTON: It would be helpful, sir, to do so in some other country.

CIC *furious and frustrated. Huge cloud of gloom and fury over the* HIPPO.

CIC: I want to look at DOG in depth. Dreadful co-ordination.

He goes. Everyone else goes, except PAGAN *and* HIPPO. PAGAN *is very upset.*

HIPPO: Send in Crago.

PAGAN *goes.*

They're conspiring. Carp's gone over. GHQ has stabbed me in the back. The Foreign Office. Up and up, as far as Anthony Eden, they are scheming, plotting, all of 'em in cahoots to hurl me into darkness, there to push a miserable pen, obscure, forgotten, stuck in the mud a *Brigadier!*

No! Never! Now I defy you long, tall pointy bastards. Arm yourselves! The Hippo's on the warpath!

He opens his briefcase and pours out a flood of blue Uncle Harry intercepts. CRAGO *comes in with his maps. So does* FIGGIS *who has a lot of files.*

HIPPO: Enemy traffic! Figgis, file it. Crago, study these. Plenty more. Do maps. Do summaries. We shall send a military mission to the partisans. Only one problem. British Foreign policy's up placed. But *Loyal!* (*Thinking furiously:*) Somebody stumpy. *Who?* (*Thinks of one.*) Got him!

CRAGO (*trying to keep abreast of developments*): Yes, sir?

HIPPO: Got him! Who do we know who can contact Winston Churchill on a personal level?

FIGGIS (*with controlled joy*): Me, you silly fool. Yes me. I know him!

HIPPO (*of her, to* CRAGO): Magnificent creature!

CRAGO *and* FIGGIS *turn their attention to the papers.*

ACT TWO

Scene One

PAGAN *and* MILA*'s apartment. The bedroom, with a door leading to a bathroom. It's nearly dawn.* PAGAN *is in bed, wearing silk pyjamas. The light is off but he is awake. The door to the hall opens and* MILA *comes in in evening-dress, trying not to make any noise.*

PAGAN: I'm awake.

MILA: What happened to you?

PAGAN: I came home. I wasn't feeling up to scratch. This arm's gone stiff.

He demonstrates: he can't move his left arm above shoulder level.

MILA: We waited for you.

PAGAN: Who is 'we'?

MILA: Oh, people from the office. Adrian. Peter Crago.

PAGAN *looks at his bedside clock.*

PAGAN: Where did you go on to?

MILA: The Mohammed Ali. I met a Captain of the Blues who owns a string of polo ponies. And he asked me very nicely if I'd do him the honour of joining him for a ride at sunrise.

PAGAN: Will you?

MILA: Shall I come to bed?

PAGAN: It's quarter to five. It's hardly worth it.

She is sitting on the bed. She touches his shoulder, massages it gently.

You're making it worse.

She gets up. Goes into the bathroom and turns on the taps. The bath is heard running. She comes in and out of the bathroom, getting undressed. Sits on a chair, undoes her suspenders and takes off her stockings. Meanwhile:

MILA: Did the Hippo bother you tonight?

PAGAN: Oh no. I'm very much out of tune with his present thinking. I'm the ancien regime, I'm tumbril fodder. He tells me nothing. Nobody does. Do you?

MILA *is in the bathroom.*

MILA (*calls out*): What?

PAGAN: What do you know about the mission to Tito?

MILA *comes back into the room.*

MILA: Only that it got the go-ahead.

PAGAN: Not from me.

MILA: Mr Churchill passed through Cairo on his way to Casablanca. And Miss Figgis pulled a string, and squeezed the Hippo in to see him between General de Gaulle and Chiang Kai-Shek.

PAGAN (*irritated*): That's what you've heard.

MILA *nods.*

In the typing pool.

She nods. Waits. He doesn't look at her. Pause.

Would you mind very much if I asked to be transferred?

MILA: What?

PAGAN: I'm being disloyal. Working for an officer I hate. Whose every triumph makes me grit my teeth in anger. It rots the soul.

MILA: What about me?

PAGAN: Mm?

MILA: Tim, you're crazy. What about my job? If you aren't working here, I'll get the chop. I'm hopeless. Where would I go? I'm Polish. I could be interned.

PAGAN: There's something I haven't told you. I attended a meeting at GHQ. I was asked a question, and I lied. One doesn't lie to men like that. It cuts across everything we're fighting for. And the Hippo's to blame. I really do think, if I stay I might attack him.

MILA: Because you lied?

He nods.

When I was travelling through Europe, I lied a hundred times a day. In a city where I'd never been before, I'd lie with the way I walked. Firm, purposeful. I always arrived on market days, so I could lose myself in the crowd. Trying to remember which of my papers I was carrying. Was I Communist, Nazi, Jew? All lies. I wore a cushion in my dress so often, so they'd think I was pregnant, that my periods stopped. It's true! Once on a station, the military policeman said, 'Your visa's lapsed, any other day of the year you'd be arrested'. I laughed as though I understood. Then I looked at the visa. Whoever it had been, it was her birthday. I was always lucky. Several times, my life was saved by my Manchurian visa. And it said I was the rabbi Shumsky, fortunately in Japanese. I loved that visa. It was so ridiculously untruthful.

PAGAN: You enjoyed it?

MILA: Yes.

PAGAN *states the questions he hasn't dared think before, with a sense of stepping into a new and dangerous area.*

PAGAN: What did you live on? How did you eat? How did you get what you wanted, in a world where men were hostile? Were they men in uniform? *What* uniform?

MILA: I tell you one thing only. You've been honest all your life. It was a luxury you could afford. I was forced to give it up some time ago. Now you must do the same. Till the end of the war. And don't ask questions.

She goes out and turns off the bathroom taps.

PAGAN: Mila.

She calls from the bathroom.

MILA: I'm having my bath.

PAGAN: Have it afterwards.

MILA *appears in the bathroom door, naked, with a towel wrapped round her.*

MILA: What?

PAGAN: Come here.

MILA: You want me to?

He nods.

You'll keep the job? What about the Hippo?

PAGAN: I'll – I'll deceive him.

She approaches him, gets on to the bed, puts a hand under the sheet. PAGAN considers the difficulties of deceiving the HIPPO:

It isn't the sort of thing I'm very good at.

MILA: What are you good at, Tim?

Scene Two

The yard at the back of the DOG offices. An empty space. Night. Darkness.

PETER CRAGO is seen above, at the first-floor window of the HIPPO's office. He lowers a rope, then glides down it with reasonable skill. (He has been training.) He hits the ground, looks around, then moves stealthily to the centre of the yard. He moves with his commando walk: coiled, alert. He waits.

From out of sight, somebody is heard whistling a bird-call. CRAGO whistles in return. The HIPPO appears out of the darkness.

HIPPO: Greetings, comrade. No sign of our task force?

CRAGO: No sir.

HIPPO: Any excuse?

CRAGO: The problem, sir, of getting them into town unrecognised –

HIPPO: Quite so, quite so. They will arrive by covert means! (*He looks about him with relish.*) Magnificent night for the job, eh? Sliver of moon. Dark shadows. And the New Year beano in the map room should divert attention. (*He produces a vehicle key from his pocket.*) Key to the truck. Don't move.

He goes off stealthily. CRAGO waits. MILA, carrying a glass, comes out of the shadows.

MILA: Peter!

CRAGO: Ssh!

MILA: Come back to the party.

CRAGO: No!

MILA: I'm lonely. Talk to me, Peter. Make me laugh.

A whistle is heard out of the darkness.

What's that?

CRAGO: It's secret. Go away.

MILA: OK. I go. (*As she goes.*) I go.

She disappears cautiously into the darkness. CRAGO waits a moment. Then WOOLF and the Jugoslav volunteers appear from another direction. None of them can be distinguished from the other, as they are all disguised as Arab women in strict purdah.

WOOLF: Peter!

CRAGO: What?

WOOLF: It's us. Look. Me. Held up in the traffic.

The HIPPO appears.

HIPPO: Ssh! Which of you is Captain Woolf?

WOOLF: I'm here, sir –

HIPPO: Taskforce will disrobe.

They get out of their purdah, and when they have done so they paint their faces with black shoe-polish. The HIPPO continues meanwhile.

Final briefing. In the corner of the yard you will observe a truck. DOG supplies for the use of. You will find inside a number of boxes, marked by intended destination. Some say Greece, the rest Albania. Our object is to capture the whole bangshoot for Jugoslavia. You will bring them here. Major Crago will be stationed in my office, first floor, and he will winch them up to safety. I shall remain in the centre of the yard, right here, and simulate normal behaviour. ready?

They form into a commando-style ready-for-action group.

Count of five. Four. Three. Two. Good luck to you all. And one.

They fall to the ground and perform a very fast and efficient crawl as developed by the SAS, until they vanish in the surrounding darkness.

HIPPO: Amazing!

CRAGO: They've been waiting eighteen months for a chance like this.

CRAGO is about to go to his post above, but -

HIPPO: A taste of action. Totally transforms the man. Gut pain vanished. Mind alert. I kip in a hammock these days. In my office. Cannot desert my post in the present ferment. Old field custom. Nap for an hour. Wake at dawn. And leap to the ground, imbued each morning with sheer zip, sheer blinding purpose. Brew up a cuppa. Good strong chai. And that's my ration foodwise for the rest of the day –

A whistle is heard. CRAGO *escapes the* HIPPO *and climbs up his rope, Two Jugoslavs come in carting a box. It is attached to the rope, and* CRAGO – *who cannot be seen now – hauls it up. Meanwhile:*

Stage one complete. Crago's waiting for the signal. Two sharp tugs.

PAGAN's *voice is heard from out of sight.*

PAGAN: Mila?

All stiffen. PAGAN *appears.*

PAGAN: May I ask what –?

Two more Jugoslavs appear behind him and immobilise him in professional manner, a hand over his mouth, another over his knees, and an arm round his chest. He is forced to the floor.

HIPPO: Oh Blimey, go a bit easy eh? Release him. Back to the grind, boys.

The two Jugoslavs responsible go. The HIPPO *addresses* PAGAN *sternly:*

Now look here Colonel Pagan –

PAGAN: If you –

HIPPO: Mission to the partisans. Must have supplies. Our Greek and Albanian missions do not *need* supplies. They have been utterly indulged. I –

PAGAN: Dummett and Pincher –

HIPPO: Bugger them both! I've made them Brigadiers, what more do they want?

PAGAN: Oh I agree.

HIPPO (*doubtful of* PAGAN's *sincerity*): You do?

PAGAN: And a mission to Tito. Excellent move. Have we permission?

HIPPO *wonders for a moment whether or not to trust the newly co-operative* PAGAN. *Decides he will for the time being. As he continues, more crates are delivered and hauled up by* CRAGO *above.*

HIPPO: Churchill, when I saw him, was in the bathtub. Nursing a tumbler. 'Won't you sit down?' he said. I did. The tap end. Face to face.

I'd written a memo. Three days work. Strenuous mental effort. But he didn't read it. Laid it on the bathmat, fixed me with his pale blue eyes and asked me for a verbal rundown.

I thought, 'Hippo, you can do this. It's a wangle! Wangle away old son!' And so I did. Military state of play. Chetnik perfidy. Gallant partisans. A frank admission. 'Some, it appears, are Bolshies.' The old man frowns. Soaps his hair, then asked me: 'Are they killing Germans?' 'Yes', say I 'and vice-versa.' 'What do you want me to do?' he asks. I'm ready for this one. 'Have we permission, sir, to establish contact with the partisans?'

He looks at the Hippo sideways. Gives the bottom of his feet a scrub. And then he nodded.

PAGAN: Nodded?

HIPPO: Very slightly. *But I spotted it.* Mission accomplished! Mission in the bag old boy! Our mission to Tito!

PAGAN: Nothing in writing?

HIPPO: Nothing exists which might alert the official channels! That's the beauty of the nod, old boy. Tacit understanding between two men of equal height. And us. (*He and* PAGAN.) And them. (*The Jugoslavs.*) We few. Nobody else must twig. Our lords and masters must be caught on the hop. Crucial element of surprise! *Once* we've landed, once we're thrashing the Hun on Balkan soil, let 'em scream blue murder. I'll say 'Bollocks'. 'Cause I wangled a nod from Churchill and deployed it.

PAGAN: Do we not tell the Chiefs of Staff?

HIPPO: There will be no collaboration! *Know your enemy!* GHQ, the boys in bowler hats, half Whitehall, all the Foreign Office, everyone in Eygpt. Rank upon rank, the whole damn panoply of the great and good against us!

Splendid. Just the job. We are guerrilla-wallahs. Masters of irregular tactics. We'll survive. We'll smash those bastards!

He turns his attention to CRAGO, *in the upstairs window.*

Crago, put Colonel Pagan in the picture.

CRAGO: The mission will drop over Crnacko Polje, behind the lines of the German winter offensive. We have evidence that partisans have infiltrated back through the lines. And the Chetniks, it appears, have been collaborating –

PAGAN: When will the mission go?

CRAGO: The next full moon.

The HIPPO *interrupts, with excitement.*

HIPPO: The rank of commanding officer will be Brigadier!

CRAGO goes on with his work, out of sight.

PAGAN: Three Brigadiers?

HIPPO: Quite so, and I have found one ready-made, an Al candidate, Malthouse, Bouncer Malthouse. Dear old pal and much maligned. Carried the can for some almighty cockup.

A whistle is heard from out of sight. WOOLF is carried on by two Jugoslavs. He is hurt and angry.

WOOLF: Twisted my blasted ankle.

HIPPO: Next in command? I'll go!

He swiftly blacks his face in shoe-polish. PAGAN prepares to leave.

PAGAN: Gentlemen, thank you. Wish I could lend a hand. Too crocked. (*To the* HIPPO:) I'd like to –

HIPPO (*getting into the mood*): Hoo! Hah!

PAGAN: So sorry about the ankle, Adrian, Peter –

He squints up to see CRAGO.

HIPPO: Woo! Woah!

PAGAN goes. The HIPPO *throws himself to the ground and leaves at length in a commando crawl. He disappears into the darkness. CRAGO appears on ground level and approaches WOOLF.*

CRAGO: All right?

WOOLF: Isn't he stunning? I was walking past the lavatories this afternoon, and he came leaping out like a cuckoo-clock and pulled me in and said security was on my tail, and not to worry, he'd protect me. Truely grateful for the way I'd trained the lads up. And my organisational skills. I said I'm loving every minute. And I meant it. Gosh, I meant it.
  You ought to be at your post.

PAGAN's voice is heard calling: 'Mila!'

CRAGO: She's up there.

WOOLF: Who?

CRAGO: Mila. In the Hippo's office. Wants to help. I let her pull the crates up. She's incredibly strong. I'm crazy about her. God it's awful. Tim's so bloody decent. Look how nice he was about your ankle.

WOOLF: Know what I think? You should. Go to bed, I mean, with whoever it is one happens to be in love with. I've come to see it as a totally unalienated human action. And anyway, it's such fun.

They sit and think about this for a moment. From the direction of the offices, the sounds of 'Auld Acquaintance' are heard CRAGO and WOOLF look at their watches.

Will you be going on the mission?

CRAGO: Well I can't say.

WOOLF: I bet you are, though.

He indicates the unseen Jugoslavs.

What about them?

CRAGO: We'll choose those men with family links in the target area.

WOOLF: Jelko?

CRAGO: Cannot confirm it. Cannot deny. I'm sorry.

A whistle is heard from out of sight. CRAGO disappears up the rope.

WOOLF: Duty calls.

The HIPPO reappears with the Jugoslavs, carrying a large crate. At the same time, MISS FIGGIS appears carrying a bottle of whisky.

FIGGIS: It's after midnight. Such a shame to let it pass unnoticed. And I've saved up this –

She produces the whisky.

HIPPO: Most welcome!

FIGGIS: – And this signal has arrived from London.

HIPPO: Let me see –

He opens and reads. The others go on working without him. MISS FIGGIS and WOOLF watch him.

Oh Crikey.

FIGGIS: What?

HIPPO: We're blown. He's rumbled us.

WOOLF: Who?

FIGGIS: Not Hitler?

HIPPO: No, no, no, the big one. Anthony Eden.

He reads the rest quickly.

WOOLF: What will he do?

FIGGIS: Please, tell us!

HIPPO: He is immobilised. We have won! The mission to Tito has official sanction, thanks to, and I quote 'the personal interest of Mr Churchill'.

FIGGIS: Splendid!

HIPPO: Hold it! Now you've got me worried. 'Personal interest'. Smacks of empire building. No, I don't think so. 'Cause he has presented us with a commanding officer.

WOOLF: Who?

HIPPO: *Not* Bouncer Malthouse. Back to the knackers yard for *him*. No this is somebody else. (*He can't remember.*) A Captain. But he won't stay a captain long! Brigadier or die!

WOOLF: His *name*?

HIPPO: Don't rush me. (*Looks at the letter. Reads*:) Bothwell.

FIGGIS: Francis Bothwell?

HIPPO: Heard of him?

FIGGIS: His father's Hamish Bothwell, Chairman of the Bank of Scotland.

HIPPO (*suppresses his extreme irritation*): That isn't his fault.

FIGGIS: Oh, quite.

HIPPO: I'm trying to like the bastard. Height?

FIGGIS: One couldn't exactly tell from the photos.

HIPPO (*irate*): Photos where?

FIGGIS: *The Times*, I think, and the *Daily Mail*.

HIPPO: What was he doing in the blasted papers?

FIGGIS: It started with the plot to abduct the Kaiser.

HIPPO: Kaiser Bill?

FIGGIS: Why, yes. As you will know, until last year he lived in peaceful exile near the Hague. He was none too pleased when the Nazis invaded Holland, and the plan was this: to get him to London and put him in charge of a German Government-in-exile. Captain Bothwell got him as far as Amsterdam, and they were about to board a fishing smack for Cleethorpes when an SS guard mistook Kaiser for the Duke of Gloucester, raised the alarm and the Kaiser died of a heart attack. All hushed up of course.

HIPPO: And Bothwell escaped?

FIGGIS: From Colditz, twelve months later.

HIPPO (*disgusted*): If Winston Churchill had scoured the earth, he could hardly have found an officer more designed to send my monkey up the pole.

WOOLF: Still, he's prime promotion fodder, wouldn't you say, sir?

HIPPO: True! I'll give him a chance.

The Jugoslavs are finished. they line up.

JELKO: Mission accomplished, Comrade Brigadier.

HIPPO: Captain Woolf.

WOOLF (*tetchy*): I'm here.

HIPPO: Prepare a tactical retreat.

WOOLF (*putting his purdah on*): I *am* doing.

HIPPO: A new year's dawning! Hope! Horizons! (*To* FIGGIS:) Pass the goblet!

FIGGIS *circulates the whisky.*

Tell me – Woolf, for starters – what do you want from the coming year?

WOOLF: I'm sorry, sir. I was never any good at games.

The Jugoslavs encourage him.

I hope that history will take its course. Specifically us. Our mission. That it gets there safely.

HIPPO: Figgis?

FIGGIS: Is this a personality test of some kind? Then I won't say Victory. Far too obvious. Peace, of course. I hope the Reading Room at the British Museum survives the war. And I'd like to run it. Next?

HIPPO: Where's Crago?

WOOLF: Mopping up, sir.

HIPPO (*of the Jugoslavs*): Speak! The proletariat!

LUKA: Knock Jerry out of the ring –

BOGDAN: A new world order –

HIPPO: You! The shy one!

JELKO: Regarding our king in exile. At the end of the war, we want a plebiscite, whole of the country, so's the people of Jugoslavia can say if they want him or not. And –

HIPPO (*rises above this*): What I hope for – don't laugh. I've a lot in here – (*Thumps his heart with deep emotion. Rises. Chooses his words with care.*) – and it's all bunged up. Dignity for all. And men walk proud. Respect. And justice. Brotherhood. And yes, it could be like that. It's up to us.

FIGGIS (*quietly to* WOOLF): Personally I blame the pills.

The Jugoslavs slap the HIPPO's *back and shake his hand in support and affection.*

HIPPO: What we should do, for luck and making it all come true, is somebody tall and dark, a stranger, enter. In a perfect world he'd carry a lump of coal. Who's game?

FRANCIS BOTHWELL *appears above at the window of the* HIPPO's *office. He is tall, dark and very handsome. He wears the uniform of a Brigadier. He is 26.*

BOTHWELL: Is Brigadier Gore down there?

HIPPO (*stares*): Who's that?

BOTHWELL: I'm Francis Bothwell.

HIPPO (*to the others*): Scarper!

They go. BOTHWELL *travels to ground level with amazing grace and speed. He approaches the* HIPPO *who pumps his hand and greets him with wild abandon.*

BOTHWELL: I tried your office –

HIPPO: Empty!

BOTHWELL: No -

HIPPO (*not listening*): I burst the bars! To roam the glorious wide and open. I'm the Hippo!

PAGAN *is heard out of sight, calling:*

PAGAN: Mila!

BOTHWELL *has been staring at* HIPPO's *face, which is still painted with black boot-polish.*

HIPPO (*paranoid*): Something the matter?

BOTHWELL: No –

HIPPO: Good, good, because I thought for a moment you were looking at me in a funny way. Ah, Pagan –

PAGAN *has appeared.*

HIPPO: – distinguished visitor. Francis Bothwell. Who's for the amber fluid?

He looks for the whisky.

PAGAN (*to* BOTHWELL): Excuse our informality. Festive season.

BOTHWELL: Seems to be catching.

PAGAN: Is it?

He sees the whisky bottle and picks it up. Meanwhile:

BOTHWELL: Yes. I just barged in on two of your staff who were seeing the New Year in with rather a bang in the Brigadier's hammock.

PAGAN: Oh my God!

The HIPPO *spots the whisky bottle.*

HIPPO: Ah ha! The culprit! (*Seizes it.*) Thank you, vicar. (*To* BOTHWELL:) A wee libation?

He passes the bottle to BOTHWELL. PAGAN's *distress becomes apparent to* BOTHWELL, *adding to the general impression of mental unbalance. Meanwhile:*

Quite a turnup for the books your popping up, old chap, and I'm glad to have had the chance to assess your character. And I like the cut of your jib. Heard lots about you. And I didn't like it. So I shall expunge it from the slates of memory. I bring you tidings of an elevating nature. You will – (*He stares at* BOTHWELL's *uniform.*) Why are you dressed as a Brigadier?

BOTHWELL: I am one.

HIPPO: I have not yet promoted you!

BOTHWELL: I saw the PM at Chequers last weekend, and *he* promoted me.

HIPPO: Oh, thank the Lord! (*He is moved with the joy of having achieved the almost unattainable.*) He told you about our little meeting did he?

BOTHWELL: Yes, he –

HIPPO: 'Cause I laid it on with a trowel about the Tito boys.

BOTHWELL: He said you stirred his heart with tales of preternatural valour.

HIPPO (*thrilled*): Thank you.

BOTHWELL: And he wants you to know that the mission will have the highest possible status. I shall be the PM's personal emissary to the partisans. I shall report direct to Number 10 –

HIPPO: And Cairo.

BOTHWELL: Oh indeed, the Commander-in-Chief himself. DOG will supply and brief me, and will be given every assistance from GHQ –

HIPPO: Hold your horses. Are you not on DOG establishment?

BOTHWELL: I am on GHQ establishment.

HIPPO (*a matter of life and death*): But you are, are you not, under my command?

BOTHWELL: Not technically. Not in practise either. I should make that clear.

HIPPO: You will take that statement back, before I sing a very different tune.

BOTHWELL: Swanee River perhaps?

The HIPPO stops in his tracks. A terrible thought strikes him. He puts his hand up to his face, touches it, and looks at the black on his fingers. Looks hard at BOTHWELL, then makes a decision.

HIPPO: You are unsuitable for the post. You will never go to Jugoslavia. Nobody at DOG will brief you. You will receive no maps, no summaries, no supplies, no men, no transport. Got the picture?

BOTHWELL (*far from being bothered by this*): Yes. (*Laughs.*) Fascinating. Wouldn't have missed it. Goodnight. (*To PAGAN:*) Rum do, Colonel. Goodnight to you.

He goes, whistling 'Way down upon the Swanee River'. The HIPPO's stomach gives him a sharp and unexpected twinge. He clutches his abdomen.

HIPPO: Oh, Christ.

He takes a swig of the whisky. Waits for the slug to knock out the pain. It doesn't. He drinks again.

PAGAN: Don't hog it, old boy

The HIPPO gives him the bottle. PAGAN drinks. The HIPPO watches him. PAGAN gives him the bottle back.

HIPPO: Can I trust you, Pagan? Over and over I pop myself the question. Are you a pal?

He gives PAGAN the bottle. PAGAN drinks.

What're you thinking? What do you, *what do you want from the war in the year to come*?

PAGAN (*chooses his words*): To destroy the enemy.

HIPPO: Bully. You're coming on. I'll tell you a secret. If we want to beat the Germans, and its clear you do, it is imperative that we beat the British first. Starting with Bothwell. How would it be if we briefed him for the Tito mission, flew him out and dropped him to the Chetniks?

PAGAN: Would we not get a splapdash reputation?

HIPPO: True. (*Thinks.*) I've got it. Nobble his parachute. Out of the hatch and down he sails and *splat*.

PAGAN (*secretly appalled*): I –

HIPPO: As you were. The bastard's sly. Whichever parachute we offer him, he'll choose another. We'd have to nobble the lot for the sake of safety. And we can't have the whole damn mission going splat. (*Has an idea.*) Or can we?

PAGAN: I have a better idea. A wangle. Do you know Whiteworks?

HIPPO: Rumour-spreading outfit?

PAGAN: That's the fellow. Whiteworks is run by a very dear friend of mine from – happier days. One Toby Jenifer. Highly connected. Ear of the CIC. And Toby and I have a long-outstanding lunch appointment.

HIPPO: Well?

PAGAN: I shall revive it. You will meet him. You will ask him to spread a rumour concerning Bothwell. Something that would make him unemployable. Make it up.

HIPPO: One snag

PAGAN: What's that?

HIPPO: He won't believe a vulgar toad like me.

PAGAN: Toby and I were fellow-bankers. I'll make up a third at lunch, and you will follow my lead precisely. He'll believe you then.

HIPPO: You're on.

PAGAN (*raising the bottle in a toast*): Let battle commence!

Scene Three

Out of the end of the previous scene, a hotel dining table becomes visible, beautifully laid for lunch. Waiters bring chairs. PAGAN and HIPPO converge on the table from opposite sides and take their places. PAGAN is ill and drunk but lucid.

TOBY JENIFER is seated between them. Smartly dressed waiters hover in attendance.

A pause. JENIFER and PAGAN have already given the waiter their orders it seems. The HIPPO is puzzling over the menu and its unfamiliar terminology.

JENIFER: Try the asparagus.

HIPPO: Where's that?

PAGAN *points it out on the menu.*

No, I don't think so. Shoot my gut to buggery sad to say. Normally I would be munching a double whisky in the Long Bar, would I not, Colonel Pagan?

PAGAN: Oh, indeed.

JENIFER (*with irony*): Indeed.

PAGAN (*to* JENIFER): How is Patricia?

JENIFER *is riveted by the HIPPO who, hot and ill at ease, is unbuttoning his tunic down the front.*

Isn't she called Patricia?

JENIFER: She's, ah, helping out at a works canteen in Peckham.

PAGAN: Bloody good show.

He continues, while the HIPPO takes his tunic off, revealing his dirty vest.

Now Margaret, as Patricia might have told you, married her airline pilot. Cleaned me out, except for some shares she didn't know about and the house in Suffolk. Went through hell, old boy, and then my luck went zing, I landed not precisely on my feet, let's say on more erotic parts of my anatomy.

JENIFER: How's the work, Tim?

PAGAN (*meaningfully, of the* HIPPO): See for yourself, eh? (*To the* HIPPO:) How're we doing?

HIPPO (*who is reading the menu again*): I'm cogitating, thank you. Don't mind me.

PAGAN (*to* JENIFER): How's yours?

JENIFER (*this is his party piece*): The job? Rather like training whippets, I imagine. One selects the rumour, mucky little creature, strokes its fur, and then one whacks it on the tail and off it shoots, and if it's a good 'un, it'll have made it twice round the town by sunset.

HIPPO (*with bogus spontaneity*): That reminds me, doesn't it, Colonel Pagan –

PAGAN: Order your lunch –

HIPPO: I will. In time. It's urgent business. Highly confidential, so *we shall not need the monkey suit brigade.*

The WAITERS, *taking the hint, melt away.*

(*To* JENIFER:) Francis Bothwell. Know him?

PAGAN (*to* JENIFER): Hamish's eldest.

JENIFER: Yes. I understand he's bound for the Balkans.

HIPPO: No, no, no, wrong end of the stick entirely. Bloody almighty cockup and it cannot happen.

JENIFER: Why?

PAGAN: The Brigadier feels he has a personality defect.

JENIFER: Has he?

HIPPO: Yes he has, and I want it put about.

JENIFER: May I ask your authority?

HIPPO: No.

JENIFER (*annoyed*): Well, you'd better tell me what the defect is.

HIPPO: He's arrogant. Looks at people in a sarky fashion.

JENIFER (*relieved that nothing very damaging is involved*): Bothwells have been pleased with themselves since the battle of Bannockburn with ample reason.

HIPPO: You'll spread it about then?

JENIFER: If you insist. I hardly think it will cut much ice.

HIPPO: You don't?

JENIFER: Why should it?

PAGAN (*to the* HIPPO): Perhaps you should explain the reason.

JENIFER: What's that?

HIPPO: Glug trouble. Jekyll and Hyde. Civil enough when he's sober, then the drink starts talking, Daily occurance. In my office. Puking, legless, half-delirious. Imagine the shock to my calm and thoughtful Jugoslavs when he's poured out over the snows in that condition.

JENIFER (*relieved once more*): Paratroopers aren't selected for their sobriety. It's their courage which matters.

PAGAN: Quite.

JENIFER: Are you trying to tell me something?

The HIPPO *looks calculatingly at* PAGAN, *who nods at him in encouragement, and then looks away, whistling a phrase of 'Swanee River'.*

HIPPO: This is the nub, old boy. And it goes against the grain to talk about a brother-officer behind his back but here it is. He's yellow. That Kaiser caper. Bothwell panicked. Gibbered. Drooled with fear.

JENIFER *weighs this statement for its probability, with distaste.*

JENIFER: Are you listening, Tim?

PAGAN: Hung on each word, old bean. It's no use gawping. Do as he says or tell him you don't believe a word.

JENIFER: Whether I believe it isn't the point. (*Is suddenly appalled.*) It hadn't crossed my mind that I was *meant* to. I imagined you were cooking up some necessary fiction. My objection was a

practical one, that nobody else would believe it either. Am I being told that this extraordinary farrago is the truth?

HIPPO: Are we?

JENIFER: Aren't we?

HIPPO (*catches* PAGAN's *drift*): No.

JENIFER (*outraged*): Then I confess I am appalled. And I must tell you, Brigadier, I saw Francis Bothwell eighteen months ago on his father's estate, when he was sober and of splendid character. Can you explain the paradox?

HIPPO: Brain deterioration.

JENIFER: What?

HIPPO: Worse each year. Age of thirty, chap'll be a parsnip. (*Taps his nose.*) Syph. And that is *fact.*

JENIFER (*convinced*): Good God.

HIPPO: You'll put it about, eh?

JENIFER: Certainly not!

HIPPO: Now look here, Colonel Whiteworks –

JENIFER: Jenifer –

HIPPO: Jenifer Whiteworks, that's an order!

JENIFER *resigns himself to this awful task.*

JENIFER: Very well. Nothing to eat, I think. (*He prepares to go. To* PAGAN:) We shall meet no doubt. I think you should see a doctor. (*Reflects:*) Poor Francis. What a terrible trick of fate. To face disease and death for a natural indiscretion which we've all committed.

HIPPO: Speak for yourself.

JENIFER: Surely you must have –

HIPPO: Not with a bloke!

JENIFER: Did you say – ?

HIPPO: Feller's a bender. Caught it off some big buck nigger with a twelve-inch cock.

JENIFER *doesn't believe this for a moment. Casts his mind back over the syphilis story. Doesn't believe that either. Doesn't believe anything he's been told. He is ice-cold angry. The* HIPPO *continues oblivious.*

Get the picture?

JENIFER: I believe I do.

HIPPO: Makes one ashamed to be an Englishman.

JENIFER: I should think it might.

HIPPO: And you'll –

JENIFER: Put it about? You may rest assured I shall report this conversation to the highest quarters. Good day to you both.

He goes. Something about his tone worries the HIPPO. *He rubs his stomach.*

HIPPO: Funny. Seemed a bit miffed.

PAGAN: You're rumbled.

HIPPO: Eh?

PAGAN: You're finished.

HIPPO: How?

PAGAN: Because you cannot lie to a man like that about a man like that. Not if you're not a man like that yourself. Not if you're you.

The HIPPO *rises in panic. Looks around for* JENIFER, *who has gone.*

HIPPO: You led me on, you – (*With dread*:) Lord. Oh Lord. If I weren't such a vulgar toad I would have known. I trusted you and you betrayed me.

PAGAN: Everything I believed in is betrayed. Honour. Rank. My colonel's flash of course was a mere convenience. How do I know, quite simple, it's like any office, one must sleep with a secretary. That's the other thing. My marriage. Utterly destroyed, except for the bed thing. Cannot explain this blooming of desire and, yes, ability, I'm forty-three for God's sake, what can I do except to welcome it and hope it lasts, but as for the rest, a nightmare. How can I love a woman I cannot trust? She only has to move a saucer and I shudder, cannot share a place at table with *my wife* – (*He shouts at the* HIPPO:) Do you see what I'm trying to say? I lied to men I respect because of you. At GHQ. Funds for the Chetnik mission.

HIPPO: You muggins. Call yourself a liar? Not in their league, old boy. They knew. Except for the CIC. 'Cause they believe what their Uncle Harry tells them.

PAGAN: You're saying that men in high positions knew the Chetniks were collaborating, yet did nothing? Knew the real resistance and ignored it?

HIPPO: That's what they're like.

MILA *approaches the table.*

MILA: Tim.

PAGAN *sees her.*

Have you finished your lunch?

HIPPO(*to* MILA): He's yours. All yours. You're welcome.

He is about to leave.

PAGAN: Hippo.

HIPPO: Well?

PAGAN: You're right, of course. It's obvious.

The HIPPO *nods and goes.*

MILA: I was worried about you. We were bringing a man from the station and we passed the hotel and I – I can't stay long.

PAGAN: Don't go.

Pause.

Would you like a raspberry ice?

MILA: You're mad.

PAGAN: I am. Completely. I love you.

She looks as if she's about to say something.

Just don't say anything.

He feels his arm. It's stiff and painful.

PAGAN: Who were you meeting at the station?

MILA: A partisan.

PAGAN: A real one?

She nods

Bring him in.

MILA: You're seeing him later. Four o'clock. You're vetting him for the mission. You remember nothing.

PAGAN: I'm incredibly drunk. And feeling ghastly. And I've never seen a partisan before, so get him.

She kisses him, goes. PAGAN *looks for a drink, tries any available bottles.*
MR DJORDEJEVIC *is brought in by a*

WAITER, *who doesn't try very hard to conceal his contempt for this shabby and unassuming figure.* DJORDEJEVIC *carries a folder which he gives to* PAGAN.

PAGAN: Sit down please. Mr –

DJORDEJEVIC: Djordejevic.

He sits.

PAGAN: You've been sent to us by the War Office, who discovered you in Wandsworth Prison.

DJORDEJEVIC: I was comfortable.

PAGAN: We're looking for men to fight in Jugoslavia. What are your skills?

DJORDEJEVIC: I was a cinema-projectionist in peace-time. Then, a partisan.

PAGAN: A partisan? (*He looks at* DJORDEJEVIC *with interest. Then looks at* DJORDEJEVIC'*s file.*) Yes. Engagements with the enemy. Prisoner in a German labour camp in Norway. From which you escaped. (*Once more he looks at* DJORDEJEVIC.) Unaided?

DJORDEJEVIC: No. My friend was with me: Radomir Boscovic. He and I were taking coffee to the workleader. We carry it through a wood. The SS guard come with us. We hit him. Boscovic take him by the throat, the gun of the SS officer is beside them. I pick it up and I run ahead. I say to myself, to disperse is better tactic. The truth is, I am afraid. When I am out of sight, I hear the shouts of men arrive, then shootings.

PAGAN: You betrayed your friend?

DJORDEJEVIC: I was weak. I do better next time. The struggle is right. The struggle will make me strong. You understand me, sir?

Slight pause.

PAGAN: In which of the following dialects are you fluent?

DJORDEJEVIC: Yes?

PAGAN *cries. Can't stop. Bends over the table, puts his head in his hands and sobs.*

Scene Four

England. 1948. A table laid for breakfast. MISS FIGGIS *is drinking a cup of tea, and doing the crossword in the* Observer. WOOLF *comes in. He has just got up.*

WOOLF: 'Morning.

FIGGIS: Hello, Adrian. Do I wish you a happy Easter?

WOOLF: If you like. Where are our hosts?

FIGGIS: Oh, up and about. Do you want the *Observer.*

WOOLF: Thank you.

She gives him the paper. He reads.

FIGGIS: Did you sleep well?

WOOLF: Somebody came in very late last night.

FIGGIS: Me, I'm afraid. I'd been to midnight mass in the village. A nice little Suffolk church. And coming back, I lost the path. Went splashing through the fields. Tim showed me a photo once in Cairo, taken, oh, before the war. The house was set in grazing land in those days. But it's sugar beet now, and sprouts.

MILA *comes in with a small basket. She is pregnant. She and* MISS FIGGIS *have seen each other already this morning.*

MILA: Happy Easter, Adrian. (*To* MISS FIGGIS:) See what I made.

MISS FIGGIS *looks in the basket.*

FIGGIS: What are they?

MILA: Eggs!

MISS FIGGIS *take one out of the basket. It has been painted in an ornate pattern.*

FIGGIS: Do we eat them?

MILA: It's a Polish custom. Adrian, look!

CRAGO *comes in. He has been working in the garden, and his wellington boots are muddy. He greets* WOOLF.

CRAGO: Good morning.

WOOLF: You're looking very agricultural.

CRAGO *puts his arms around* MILA.

CRAGO: We're living off the land, aren't we, my darling?

WOOLF: I'm going back to bed in a minute.

MILA: You're meant to be writing a book.

FIGGIS: He is. He comes up to the British Museum twice a week.

WOOLF: Figgis gives me special treatment.

FIGGIS: I do not. I'ver merely introduced a proper system. All our readers benefit.

MILA: Eat!

They crack their decorated eggs and eat. After a while.

CRAGO: Adrian wants to pick my brains.

WOOLF: I'm researching the Cairo chapter.

FIGGIS: Well it's no use asking us. We were cogs, that's all. All we saw was what we were working on. None of us knew the overall picture. So we forget what the war was like. We remember rumours and think they happened. None of them did.

MILA: One did.

FIGGIS: Oh, what?

MILA: The same time Peter went to Jugoslavia. Tim was ill. He used to – cry at his desk. We used to say to men who came for interviews, 'anything strange that Colonel Pagan does, pay no attention, it's his way of testing how you will react in unusual circumstances'. Next day he saw a man for a job in Greece. Half-way through the interview, Tim go pale and fall to the floor. The man think, oh this is an easy one. He sit and watch. Tim die.

Pause.

WOOLF: Do you dine out on that?

CRAGO: She's never mentioned it.

FIGGIS: Surely the Hippo was involved? I heard, he'd called in Whiteworks, and told the most terrible lies about Brigadier Dummett.

WOOLF: No it was Bothwell.

CRAGO: I heard, Brigadier Pincher –

WOOLF: Whoever it was, it all links up. Because when poor old Tim got wind of it, he had an apoplectic fit. I mean, quite literally. And that's what killed him.

MILA: Tim was killed because he knew too much.

FIGGIS: By whom?

MILA: The Russians.

WOOLF: Phooey!

MILA (*angry*): Tim was a hero! A hero!

Pause.

WOOLF: The greatest fantasy, of course, was Peter's about the partisans.

CRAGO: I know what I saw. The heroism of the men and women there. And what they were fighting against was evil. So the war was right. It was a total moral certainty, which I hadn't felt in Cairo to put it mildly. And the partisans won. And formed a government, which I support.

WOOLF: Unreservedly?

CRAGO: Yes, when you're around.

WOOLF: Never confuse the leadership with the rank and file. We all like sturdy peasants. We even love them. What's irresponsible, Peter, and sentimental of you, is to exploit them for the benefit of the Tito regime. Which is an utterly bourgeois, petty-nationalistic oligarchy. And if the Soviet Union chucked it out tomorrow and set up a workers' state, it would be right, quite right.

Pause. CRAGO angry.

MILA: I'm not happy Peter helped the Reds.

CRAGO *so angry he can't think of anything to say. Pushes his egg away. Pause.* FIGGIS *changes the subject with tact.*

FIGGIS: Does anyone know what happened to the Hippo?

It seems that nobody does.

Scene Five

The HIPPO alone with a suitcase. Lightning and a clap of thunder.

HIPPO: I've made a vital discovery. (*He puts his luggage down. Takes out his canister of pills. Takes a pill. Reads the label.*) 'Take in moderation'. Bollocks. Nothing puts me out. Not gas. Not chloroform. (*Another flash of lightning, and simultaneously a clap of thunder, both of which he receives as tedious reminders from above.*) Yes, yes, yes, I've got it. Who's that? (*He has seen a figure in the encircling darkness. It is* CARP.) It's you, Carp. What do you want? Where am I?

CARP: Cairo airfield.

HIPPO: Am I? So I am. (*He shakes his head as though awakening from sleep. He looks around. He is indeed at the airfield. Lights twinkle and aeroplanes are heard revving up. The* HIPPO's *attention settles on* CARP.) You betrayed me. Failed to back me up on the Chetnik question. 'Nuff said. I've had a quite astounding insight. Struck me in the course of a fearful meeting. Audience with the CIC. This afternoon. One Colonel Jenifer in attendance. Cutting things were said about me. Guttersnipe. A petty gangster. Morals of a chimpanzee. I didn't deny it. Have I ever? All my life I have accepted that those bastards are against me. And they *are* against me. That's the insight. Shattering. After years of patient service. Mute devotion. Grovelling. *One exception*. New Year's Eve. Young Bothwell. Could have *got* him if I'd wanted. Could have swung him under my command, there are ways and means. I'd have had my third Brigadier. Promotion. Fame and glory. And an army of one million partisans. What a fantastic prize! And I looked at Bothwell. Tall, blue-blooded, pointy hero. And I couldn't abide him. So I picked a fight and lost. A proud defeat. 'Cause I'm sick to death of being their little Lord Fauntleroy. I tell you what I am, eh, Carp, I am a damned rebellious Bolshie major, out of a job, no Uncle Harry, sitting on my only suitcase on the tarmac at the airfield while my future is decided.

CARP: That's what I've come to tell you.

HIPPO: Eh?

CARP: Your future –

HIPPO: Yes, I'm with you. Fire away.

CARP: We need a volunteer.

HIPPO (*with flicker of bravado*): Don't look at me, old boy. Never volunteered for anything in my life. Staunch principle. Unless it were extremely attractive, I might reconsider but I hae ma doots. What is it? Might one cop it? What's the chances?

CARP: Hundred per cent.

HIPPO: Ah. Well, we might just be in business, 'cause I thought for a moment it might be hazardous. Unless you – (*Alarmed*.) You don't mean – ? What?

CARP: Plans have been completed for a major assault on Europe. The landings will take place in Sicily. It is vital that the enemy is deceived. An officer is required to drive a jeep along the German lines near Tripoli, where at a pre-arranged signal it will explode. Amongst the officer's – remains – will be found the plans for a supposed invasion of Sardinia.

HIPPO (*suspicious*): When you say volunteer – ?

CARP: Oh, pukka bona fide, you can spit in my eye if you like. They simply –

HIPPO: – thought I might be interested?

CARP: Well, yes.

HIPPO: Because it's not as though you were selling it very hard.

CARP: On the positive side, in order to give the maximum weight to the document, the officer concerned will have been, so sorry, will be – a general. (*Slight pause*.) The pay is excellent and I believe the perks include –

HIPPO: I'm thinking.

He has seen somebody in a far corner of the NAAFI. CRAGO's *voice is heard:*

CRAGO: Sir!

CRAGO *appears out of the darkness. He is in full battledress in preparation for a drop.*

CRAGO: Good to see you. We heard you'd got the –

HIPPO: No no no, I am being heavily wooed. The mission's going tonight, eh?

CRAGO: In a few minutes. I'm just escaping from the Wing-Commander's hospitality.

HIPPO: There's Captain Woolf.

WOOLF *appears from another direction, dressed as usual.*

Over here! (*To* CRAGO:) He's looking bloody glum. How're your Jugs?

WOOLF: It would have been nice if they'd been allowed to drink with the sahibs. But they're fine. We've had a joyful reunion. An uncle and a long-lost nephew. Jelko, splendid chap. Thrilled to be going back home, they are. For ever, hopefully. (*He's tearful, but face quiet and calm.*) Pig of a cold.

BOTHWELL *is there at a distance, dressed for the drop.*

BOTHWELL: Major Crago.

HIPPO (*whispers to* CARP): Ah, young Lochinvar.

CRAGO: Yes, sir.

BOTHWELL: We're leaving pronto.

WOOLF (*to* CRAGO): Historic moment.

CRAGO: Yes.

WOOLF: So pleased. So very happy for you all. Take care.

WOOLF *and* CRAGO *embrace, then part in different directions. There is no-one there except for* CARP *and the* HIPPO.

CARP: Well?

HIPPO: Tell them, thanks for thinking of me but I'm not mad keen. It isn't just the rank, you see. It's what the rank implies. Being remembered. Who, in years to come, will recall a clumsy clod of a general whose only distinction was to leave this world in a bang and a puff of smoke?

CARP: They'll remember you for winning the war in Jugoslavia.

HIPPO: Will they? Did I?

CARP: Policy was wrong. We all knew that. But only you had the guts to change it.

HIPPO (*thinks for a moment, then gives credit where it's due*): Me and Winston. Perfectly true.

CARP: The only question's whether you'll be remembered as a miserable major? Or a General?

HIPPO: Sky's the limit.

He shakes CARP's *hand in agreement.*

CARP: Done.

An RAF NCO comes into sight saying 'come along, lads'. The mission follows him into sight en route to the tarmac. The Jugoslav volunteers appear from another direction. A crowd of men and officers, in full battledress and parachute harness. CRAGO *and* BOTHWELL *are among them. Some are nervous, some joking and larking about. The* HIPPO *approaches them as they pass and disappear from sight.*

HIPPO: Bothwell! No hard feelings. Bloody good luck to you. Peter! Give them hell eh? Up and at 'em? (*To another:*) Yes it's me! They booted me out for a mo' but I came bouncing back – (*To others:*) Know what they are? Up there? Top floor? A bunch of bastards. Hate me. Always have done. But they cannot do without me. Back they crawled. And I said yes. 'Cause I'm the Hippo! I'm their British backbone!

The stage is empty except: Image: apotheosis of the HIPPO: *alone, triumphant.*